The Manager's self~assessment kit

The Manager's self~*assessment kit*

A complete appraisal system for successful career development

Foreword by Lord Hanson

KOGAN PAGE

⫴ ERNST & YOUNG

First published in 1990
by Ernst & Young
This edition published in 1991
by Kogan Page Ltd

Apart from any fair dealing for the purposes of research or private study, or criticism or review, as permitted under the Copyright, Designs and Patents Act, 1988, this publication may only be reproduced, stored or transmitted, in any form or by any means, with the prior permission in writing of the publishers, or in the case of reprographic reproduction in accordance with the terms of licences issued by the Copyright Licensing Agency. Enquiries concerning reproduction outside those terms should be sent to the publishers at the undermentioned address:

Kogan Page Limited
120 Pentonville Road
London N1 9JN

© Crown copyright
This book is published by permission of The Controller of Her Majesty's Stationery Office.
The material in the book is Crown Copyright. Purchasers of the book acquire the right to make one copy for their own personal use. Copying for teaching, management development or other purposes is not permitted. Copies of individual skills profiles can be bought from Ernst & Young's Manchester office, on request.
Ernst & Young
Lowry House
Marble Street
Manchester M2 6LP

British Library Cataloguing in Publication Data
A CIP record for this book is available from the British Library.

ISBN 0-7494-0449-3

Typeset by DP Photosetting, Aylesbury, Bucks
Printed and bound in Great Britain by
Biddles Ltd, Guildford and Kings Lynn

◀ FOREWORD ▶

Lord Hanson, Chairman Hanson Plc

Successful managers are self-starters, committed to developing themselves, committed to acquiring practical skills and committed to achievement.

Hanson spends much time assessing its managers, motivating them and encouraging their development. This is fundamental to our success.

This book is aimed at helping those committed managers. As the introduction says, it is a self-assessment kit to help those who want to develop greater career success, with success being defined by them and not by the authors.

The advice given is practical and to the point. The wide range of profiles will be invaluable in helping managers to appraise their skills and then look for ways to improve them. Individual managers and company management teams will find this book of great help. It fulfils a real need. I recommend it to you.

October 1990

◀ ACKNOWLEDGEMENTS ▶

This book was produced as a result of a project sponsored by the Employment Department Training Agency. The views expressed are those of the authors and do not necessarily reflect those of the Employment Department or any other Government Department.

The authors wish to acknowledge the help of the Training Agency and in particular of Peter Reid and David Vickers, who gave support throughout its development. Colleagues within Ernst & Young, business friends and a wide range of managers in industry, commerce and the public sector, have also been of valuable assistance to us in testing the profiles and suggesting drafts or amendments.

We give particular thanks to the panel of experienced senior managers who chose the 20 personality traits used in the Personal Profile and who defined the preferred range of scores within those traits.

◀ PREFACE ▶

This book originated in work by Dr Brearley at Bradford University Management Centre, in evaluating the skills of middle and senior managers from many organisations and then helping them with their career development.

The work was further developed by Dr Brearley at Ernst & Young into a series of skills profiles which have been used widely in recruiting middle and senior managers for clients; and in developing managers in a wide range of organisations including Burmah Oil and Birmingham Airport, to name only two.

The present book is the outcome of a close collaboration over the last three years by the two authors from Ernst & Young and the Training Agency.

As the introduction says, it is intended for managers who want to develop their own careers. It can, of course, also be used by business and public sector organisations as a means of encouraging that development.

We believe that managers need all the help they can get in developing their careers. We trust that the book will contribute to that help over many years to come.

A Brearley
D Sewell
Manchester 1990

◀ CONTENTS ▶

◀ **Section 1 – Introduction** ▶	13
This Book	15
A Career	16
Three Clichés of Career Development	16
A Counsellor	17
The Book Layout	18
How to Proceed	19
◀ **Section 2 – Competence Review** ▶	21
Career and Performance Profile	23
Personal Profile	24
Personal Management Skills Profile	45
Overall Management Skills Profile	45
Functional Management Skills Profiles	45
◀ **Section 3 – Present Position Profile** ▶	47
Summary of Career and Performance Profile	49
Summary of Personal Profile	51
Summary of Management Skills Profiles	54
◀ **Section 4 – Career Planning Guide** ▶	57
Introduction	59
Your Final Post	60

Skills Analysis	61
Key Gaps	62
Gaps Summary	64
Job Progression	64
Job Progression Analysis (pro-forma)	67
Skills Progression	68
Personal Skills Profile Gaps	62
Overall Skills Profile Gaps	63
Functional Management Skills Profile Gaps	63
Improving Your Skills	71
Action Planning: Your Next Move	73
Action Planning: Longer Term	74

◀ Section 5 – Conclusion ▶   77

Success	79
Changing Views	79
Self-Development	79
Continuous Development	80
Career Choice	80
A Counsellor	80
Career and Performance Profile	80
Personal Profile	80
Skills Profiles	81
Career Planning	81
Skill Development	81
Action Plan	81

◀ Section 6 – Appendices – Management Skills Profile Questionnaires ▶   85

Profile A	– Personal Management Skills Profile	86
Profile B	– Overall Management Skills Profile	91
Profile C1	– General Management	96
Profile C2	– Business Policy	106
Profile C3	– Organising and Dealing with People	118
Profile C4	– Accounting and Finance	127
Profile C5	– Operations	142
Profile C6	– Marketing and Sales	150

Profile C7 – Research and Product Development   165
Profile C8 – Personnel and Employee Relations   178
Profile C9 – Purchasing   197
Profile C10 – Exporting   210
Profile C11 – Information Technology   225
Profile C12 – New Technology   237
Profile C13 – Retailing, Warehousing and Distribution   247

◀ **SECTION 1   INTRODUCTION** ▶

◀ **SECTION 1**

◀ INTRODUCTION ▶

THIS BOOK

This book is intended for managers who want to develop their own careers. If you are in early or mid-career, then this book is for you.

This book is very much a self-assessment kit to help you if you want to develop yourself towards greater career success; with success being defined by you, not by the authors.

This book does not set out to be:

- A manual of career opportunities, with factual information such as entry requirements, prospects, and salary ranges. A vast amount of that literature is readily available elsewhere.

- A manual of learning techniques and learning styles. Again such information is available elsewhere.

- A manual on the details of specific management skills. The range of information on those is vast, and readily obtainable. You will probably already be familiar with the material immediately relevant to your present role, and can readily research the material available as you become clearer about your future skill requirements stemming from your work with this book.

- A set of 'tests'. All the questionnaires are simple self-appraisals and are certainly not tests.

- A set of specialist questionnaires for particular industries, or sectors, although it is intended to be broadly suitable for all key management areas of industry, commerce and the public sector.

- A recommendation of any particular management style or supposed success formula.

- A set of recommendations as to what career path you should follow; that is a matter for you, the book is designed to help.

A CAREER

What do we mean by a career? *The Shorter Oxford Dictionary* says:

Career - a person's progress through life, a profession offering opportunities for advancement.

In general, the word career when applied to employment as a manager presupposes:

- a hierarchy or range of hierarchies of some kind with scope for upward progression by individual managers;

- the possibility of acquiring over time a body of knowledge, skills, and competences through study and experience;

- qualifying, in a range of ways, to be entrusted with specific kinds of management role;

- the opportunity as your reputation increases to be employed on bigger, more challenging, and more rewarding work;

- the opportunity for greater flexibility of choice, greater security, greater status, and higher rewards if those are the things you want.

THREE CLICHÉS OF CAREER DEVELOPMENT

Three clichés often heard when career development is discussed are:

- career development is self-development – this book assumes that to be true and is therefore written to help you to develop yourself and your own career;
- career development is continuous throughout your career – this book also assumes that to be true and is aimed at helping you at any stage of your career;
- career choice is a process not an event – again this book is based on that assumption. You are asked to consider your career choices at all stages of your 'life', as opportunities open up, and as other opportunities close.

A COUNSELLOR

In this book you are encouraged to analyse yourself, and your aspirations, and make career judgements which you can buttress by seeking ways of developing yourself.

That is a pretty lonely business and it really has to be. However it is extremely valuable if at the various stages of your analysis you have the help of a counsellor or mentor who can give an outside judgement of you and of your analysis, on an entirely confidential basis aimed purely at helping you.

The sort of person you want is one who:

- knows you reasonably well, and whom you regard as a candid friend;
- is a competent and successful manager in your own field or a similar field;
- is prepared to give you some time;
- is a person whose judgement you feel you can trust;
- preferably has some experience of helping managers to develop their careers;
- is prepared to help you to arrive at your conclusions rather than seek to tell you what to do.

That may seem to be a demanding specification, and indeed it is. However, there are many such people around and the right sort of person will almost invariably be pleased to give you all the help possible.

THE BOOK LAYOUT

As you will see from the contents page, this book consists of six sections.

Section 1 - Introduction
A general résumé of what the book is, how it is structured, how to use it, and how it can help you to appraise and develop your own career.

Section 2 - Competence Review
A set of profiles to enable you to review and assess your present situation and competence levels.

- A Career and Performance Profile which you will be asked to complete.

- A Personal Profile which you will be asked to complete.

- A Personal Management Skills Profile which you will be asked to complete.

- An Overall Management Skills Profile which you will be asked to complete.

- A set of 13 Functional Management Skills Profiles of which you will be asked to select one or two, or at the most three which are appropriate to you and complete them.

Section 3 - Present Position Profile

- A summary by you of the outcome of the Career and Performance Profile.

- A summary by you of the outcome of the Personal Profile.

- A summary by you of the Functional Management Skills Profiles you have selected.

These summaries add up to your view of your present position in all these matters. It is at this stage that you will begin consultations with the counsellor you have chosen.

Section 4 - Career Planning Guide
A structured analysis by you of your career aspiration, of the likely programme of jobs you see as leading to that final aspiration, and an assessment of your learning needs when comparing that progression with your Present Position Profile.

Section 5 - Conclusion
A general summary of your views and of an action plan for your future development.

Section 6 - Appendices - Management Skills Profile Questionnaires
The full set of 15 Management Skills Profile Questionnaires used for your appraisal in Section 2.

HOW TO PROCEED

It is suggested that you now:

- look forward through the book to form a general idea of its contents;

- give some thought to a person who may be suitable and willing to be your counsellor and seek to get his or her agreement;

- move to Section 2 and begin the appraisal work suggested there.

◀ SECTION 2
COMPETENCE REVIEW ▶

◄ SECTION 2

◄ COMPETENCE REVIEW ▶

We now come to the overall appraisals by you of the elements which make up your present competence levels.

CAREER AND PERFORMANCE PROFILE

The first appraisal is a Career and Performance Profile which is set out on the next eight pages. Please now turn to the next page and complete the questionnaire. Full instructions are given on those pages.

COMPETENCE REVIEW – CAREER AND PERFORMANCE PROFILE ▶

The Career and Performance Profile is the name we have given to an overall summary of:

- your personal details, career experience, training record and career achievements;
- your own appraisal of your performance in your present job;
- your own assessment of your strengths and weaknesses, career aspirations, mobility preference, and self-development plans.

What you are asked to do is to read this questionnaire, think about it, then fill it in giving careful thought at each stage and remembering that the document is your assessment and is purely for your own use.

Personal details

Surname _____ Date of birth _____

Forenames _____

Address _____

_____

_____ Children _____

_____ (Age/Sex) _____

Marital status _____

Full-time education
School(s), College, University   From   To

Part-time education
Where   From   To

COMPETENCE REVIEW ▶ 25

Qualifications
Details of professional qualifications, of whatever level, obtained by examination, and dates obtained.

Details of membership of other bodies which you regard as relevant.

Publications
Publications recognised professionally.

Training courses attended
Internal   Dates

External   Dates

Career history

Present post _____

Date of appointment (to present post) _____

Main duties performed in your present post, including number of staff controlled, and to whom you report:

Previous appointments held within your present organisation:
Post   From   To

Appointments held prior to joining your present organisation:
Company   Post   From   To

Present post
Performance review in present post
What have been the principal objectives in your present post during the last two years?

How well do you think these principal objectives have been met?

Areas of strength relevant to success in meeting those objectives.

Areas of weak performance relevant to meeting those objectives.

Overall performance summary in your present post and any other relevant factors.

Career analysis
Summary of the main achievements in your career as a whole to date.

Strengths and weaknesses
In your career to date what do you see as your main strengths and weaknesses?

Personal characteristics
Strengths   Weaknesses

Skills
Strengths   Weaknesses

COMPETENCE REVIEW ▶ 29

Satisfaction
At work, what do you enjoy doing most? What do you enjoy doing least? What do you feel about your remuneration and conditions of employment?

Satisfaction initiatives
What initiatives have you taken recently to improve your job satisfaction?

Career aspirations

Given a free choice, what would be the next job you would like to do within your present organisation, and when? If the answer is 'none' please say so; we shall be looking at your general career aspirations later in the book.

Training

In your view, what further training – internal or external – or development experience do you require:

1. to improve your performance in your present job?

2. to prepare you for progression?

Mobility

Mobility preference (describe any mobility restriction with time scales).

Self-development
Many people believe that the most effective form of development is self-development. Describe any steps you have taken, or are taking, to develop your career.

Other matters
Use this section to include any information you want to add which is not covered (or sufficiently covered) in the preceding sections.

COMPETENCE REVIEW – PERSONAL PROFILE ▶

The second appraisal is a Personal Profile which is set out on the next seven pages. Please now, as you read on, complete the questionnaire. Full instructions are given on these pages.

The Personal Profile is the title we have given to an overall summary of your personality characteristics. There are very many personality traits defined in the English language, indeed well over 4,000 trait names are in use. Obviously it would not be sensible, or indeed possible, to consider all of them. We therefore asked a panel of experienced senior managers to choose the 20 personality traits they felt were most relevant to management success.

What you will be asked to do is to evaluate yourself on each of these 20 personality traits. We emphasise that this is purely a self-assessment and is in no way a test.

Personality traits are often evaluated by means of psychometric tests administered by an occupational psychologist. There are more than 5,000 such tests available in the English language. If you want a completely dispassionate analysis of your personality then you should contact a qualified occupational psychologist and take a carefully chosen range of tests.

Nevertheless a self-appraisal is in itself a very useful aid to clarifying your own judgement of yourself, and you are now asked to make such an appraisal.

The procedure you are asked to follow is to:

- read the definitions of each of the traits which are set out below;

- think about each trait;

- score yourself on a scale from 1 to 10 for each trait;

- cross-check your scores with your counsellor, and alter your scores if you wish;

- enter your scores on the Personal Profile summary sheet given at the end of this section;

- then, and only then, compare your scores with the 'preferred' scores for managers set out in the Personal Profile Analysis. These 'preferred' scores also were chosen by our panel of experienced senior managers.

Please bear in mind that a low or a high number is not in itself a judgement; in other words, high is not necessarily desirable and low is not necessarily undesirable. Please also bear in mind that when you look at the 'preferred' scores of managers shown in the Personal Profile Analysis you should not worry if your scores differ from those, simply bear your profile in mind.

Trait 1 - *Decisiveness*

High score
A high score indicates a person who can weigh factors and readily decide on a course of action.

Low score
A low score indicates a person who has difficulty in making decisions.

1   2   3   4   5   6   7   8   9   10

Trait 2 - *Determination*

High score
A high score indicates a person who shows resolution and perseverance, and a purposeful approach.

Low score
A low score indicates a person who easily loses heart in the face of difficulties, and readily alters course.

1   2   3   4   5   6   7   8   9   10

Trait 3 - *Diplomacy*

High score
A high score indicates a person who is subtle and tactful in dealing with others.

Low score
A low score indicates a person who can be rather brash and insensitive in relationships.

1   2   3   4   5   6   7   8   9   10

Trait 4 - Drive

High score
A high score indicates a person who shows enterprise and get-up-and-go.

Low score
A low score indicates a person who is rather apathetic and unmotivated.

1   2   3   4   5   6   7   8   9   10

Trait 5 - Energy

High score
A high score indicates a person who shows forcefulness and vigour in the pursuit of objectives.

Low score
A low score indicates a person who shows little vitality and stamina, and is rather laid-back.

1   2   3   4   5   6   7   8   9   10

Trait 6 - Enthusiasm

High score
A high score indicates a person who shows eagerness and zeal.

Low score
A low score indicates a person who is not much given to keenness or earnestness, and is rather staid.

1   2   3   4   5   6   7   8   9   10

Trait 7 – Fairness

High score
A high score indicates a person who is balanced and equitable in dealings with others, and strives for impartiality.

Low score
A low score indicates a person who can be biased, unjust with other people, and not concerned with colleagues' feelings.

1   2   3   4   5   6   7   8   9   10

Trait 8 – Flexibility

High score
A high score indicates a person who is adaptable, open-minded, and responsive to change.

Low score
A low score indicates a person who can be rigid, stubborn, and not amenable to change.

1   2   3   4   5   6   7   8   9   10

Trait 9 – Foresight

High score
A high score indicates a person who looks forward and anticipates problems and opportunities.

Low score
A low score indicates a person who is not far-sighted and can thus be unprepared.

1   2   3   4   5   6   7   8   9   10

Trait 10 – *Honesty*

High score
A high score indicates a person who is ethical, law-abiding, and does not aim to deceive.

Low score
A low score indicates a person who is untrustworthy and untruthful.

1   2   3   4   5   6   7   8   9   10

Trait 11 – *Intelligence*

High score
A high score indicates a person who is alert, quick-thinking and who readily grasps new ideas.

Low score
A low score indicates a person who is slow to grasp new ideas.

1   2   3   4   5   6   7   8   9   10

Trait 12 – *Judgement*

High score
A high score indicates a person who is analytical, wise, and makes sound decisions.

Low score
A low score indicates a person who has a low level of discernment and wisdom.

1   2   3   4   5   6   7   8   9   10

Trait 13 – Leadership orientation

High score
A high score indicates a person who enjoys responsibility and actively seeks a leadership role.

Low score
A low score indicates a person who avoids taking a position of responsibility, feels uncomfortable in such a position, and tends to follow rather than lead.

1   2   3   4   5   6   7   8   9   10

Trait 14 – Logicality

High score
A high score indicates a person who approaches issues in an analytical fashion, makes decisions based on a balanced analysis, and can avoid prejudice.

Low score
A low score indicates a person whose thought processes tend to be irrational and intuitive.

1   2   3   4   5   6   7   8   9   10

Trait 15 – Loyalty

High score
A high score indicates a person who is constant, dependable and sincere.

Low score
A low score indicates a person who readily shifts allegiance and is undependable.

1   2   3   4   5   6   7   8   9   10

Trait 16 – Reliability

High score
A high score indicates a person who stands firm, is purposeful, constant and stable.

Low score
A low score indicates a person who is strongly affected by feelings and is not dependable.

1   2   3   4   5   6   7   8   9   10

Trait 17 – Resilience

High score
A high score indicates a person who is buoyant and who recovers rapidly from set backs.

Low score
A low score indicates a person who easily becomes discouraged and does not cope easily with difficulties.

1   2   3   4   5   6   7   8   9   10

Trait 18 – Self-confidence

High score
A high score indicates a person who is assured, audacious and bold.

Low score
A low score indicates a person who is fretful, a worrier and easily gets depressed.

1   2   3   4   5   6   7   8   9   10

Trait 19 – Self-control

High score
A high score indicates a person who stays steady and behaves in a calm, controlled manner.

Low score
A low score indicates a person who is strained, tense, and readily shows frustration with people and events.

1   2   3   4   5   6   7   8   9   10

Trait 20 – Stability

High score
A high score indicates a person who is calm, steady and unruffled.

Low score
A low score indicates a person who becomes erratic in conditions of stress and change.

1   2   3   4   5   6   7   8   9   10

PERSONAL PROFILE SUMMARY ▶

	1	2	3	4	5	6	7	8	9	10
Trait 1 – *Decisiveness*										
Trait 2 – *Determination*										
Trait 3 – *Diplomacy*										
Trait 4 – *Drive*										
Trait 5 – *Energy*										
Trait 6 – *Enthusiasm*										
Trait 7 – *Fairness*										
Trait 8 – *Flexibility*										
Trait 9 – *Foresight*										
Trait 10 – *Honesty*										
Trait 11 – *Intelligence*										
Trait 12 – *Judgement*										
Trait 13 – *Leadership orientation*										
Trait 14 – *Logicality*										
Trait 15 – *Loyalty*										
Trait 16 – *Reliability*										
Trait 17 – *Resilience*										
Trait 18 – *Self-confidence*										
Trait 19 – *Self-control*										
Trait 20 – *Stability*										

PERSONAL PROFILE ANALYSIS ▶

This analysis sets out the preferred scores for managers for the traits laid out in the Personal Profile.

Trait 1 - Decisiveness
A score of 7 to 9 is preferred. A low score would indicate a person who has difficulty weighing factors and making decisions. It is just about possible to be too decisive which could indicate an impetuousness in decision-making, and this is taken into account by not preferring a score as high as 10.

Trait 2 - Determination
A score of 6 to 9 is preferred. Too low a score would indicate a person who loses heart and readily alters course. A score at the very top of the scale could indicate a person who perseveres even when there is no hope of a successful outcome.

Trait 3 - Diplomacy
A score of 4 to 8 is preferred. Too low a score indicates a certain brashness and insensitivity in dealings with others. A score above 8 can indicate a level of subtlety and tact which is rather excessive for management success.

Trait 4 - Drive
A score of 6 to 8 is preferred. A low score indicates apathy and lack of motivation. A score above 8 could indicate a person whose drive is so strong that colleagues find it very hard to live with and to support, thus possibly leading to team disruption.

Trait 5 - Energy
A score of 5 to 9 is preferred. A low score indicates lack of vitality and stamina. At a score above 9, the energy level can be excessive for management team effectiveness.

Trait 6 - Enthusiasm
A score of 7 to 9 is preferred. A low score would indicate insufficient keenness for managerial success. Too high a score could indicate a tendency to get carried away when an attractive course of action is available.

Trait 7 – Fairness
A score of 4 to 8 is preferred. A low score indicates a person who is unjust. Too high a score can result in giving the good treatment of others too high a priority.

Trait 8 – Flexibility
A score of 5 to 9 is preferred. Too low a score indicates rigidity and probably an unwillingness to change. Too high a score can indicate a person who vacillates and is too ready to change course.

Trait 9 – Foresight
A score of 5 to 9 is preferred. A low score indicates a person who is not far-sighted and thus can be unprepared. Too high a score could indicate a person who foresees every nuance of difficulty in future issues thus leading to problems in taking decisions.

Trait 10 – Honesty
A score of 8 to 10 is preferred. In other words we expect a manager to be scrupulously honest in dealings and have a high level of intellectual honesty. The lower score of 8 simply indicates that perfection is not always attainable.

Trait 11 – Intelligence
A score of 6 to 9 is preferred. High levels of intelligence are vital to managerial success, at too low a score there are obvious risks of failure of comprehension and analysis.

Trait 12 – Judgement
A score of 7 to 9 is preferred. A manager needs to be analytical, wise, and make sound decisions. Below a score of 7 there are likely to be problems with unsound decisions. It is scarcely possible to have too high a score, the top bracket of 9 simply recognises realities.

Trait 13 – Leadership orientation
A score of 6 to 9 is preferred. A low score indicates a person who follows rather than leads. A high score is very desirable. At the very highest score, however, leadership orientation can be so high that difficulties working in a team can ensue.

Trait 14 – *Logicality*

A score of 7 to 9 is preferred. Logical decision-making is important in management and a high score is essential. At the very highest score, however, logicality can become rigidity and a refusal to let any element of intuition intrude at all.

Trait 15 – *Loyalty*

A score of 5 to 8 is preferred. Too low a score indicates a person who is not dependable. Too high a score can mean that a person remains loyal upwards or downwards beyond the point at which such loyalty becomes unreasonable in the light of the actual situation.

Trait 16 – *Reliability*

A score of 7 to 10 is preferred. No level of reliability can be too high in management. The lower score simply indicates that perfection is unlikely.

Trait 17 – *Resilience*

A score of 7 to 9 is preferred. A person with a low score who easily becomes discouraged and does not cope with difficulties is clearly not suitable for management. High levels of buoyancy and the ability to recover from setbacks are essential.

Trait 18 – *Self-confidence*

A score of 6 to 9 is preferred. At too low a score worry and fretfulness are a problem. At a score above 9, a person could be overconfident and thus rather rash.

Trait 19 – *Self-control*

A score of 5 to 9 is preferred. A low score indicates a person who shows frustration with people and events, and can be strained and tense. Too high a score can indicate an over-controlled person who never shows feelings at all and can be regarded by colleagues as cold and unfeeling, which can be a problem in management.

Trait 20 – *Stability*

A score of 6 to 9 is preferred. Too low a score indicates a person who is erratic. At the very highest score there could be a problem of unwillingness to face the reality of the need to change in the face of circumstances.

COMPETENCE REVIEW – PERSONAL MANAGEMENT SKILLS PROFILE ▶

The third appraisal is a Personal Management Skills Profile which is set out as Profile A in Section 6 of this book on pages 86 to 90. Please now turn to that profile and complete the questionnaire. Full instructions are given in the profile.

COMPETENCE REVIEW – OVERALL MANAGEMENT SKILLS PROFILE ▶

The fourth appraisal is an Overall Management Skills Profile which is set out as Profile B in Section 6 of this book on pages 91 to 95. Please now turn to that profile and complete the questionnaire. Full instructions are given in the profile.

COMPETENCE REVIEW – FUNCTIONAL MANAGEMENT SKILLS PROFILES ▶

As you will have seen, Profile B the Overall Management Skills Profile in Section 6 covers a range of areas of skill and knowledge required in the management of a business.

You are now asked to go into rather more detail by choosing one or two, or at the most three of those areas and complete a further questionnaire on those. The full range of Functional Management Skills Profiles is set out in the appendix to this book as Profiles C1 to C13 starting on page 96.

How should you make a choice of the Functional Management Skills Profiles? The following approach is suggested.

- First choose the skills profile which covers your present functional skills area, eg if you are an accountant choose Profile C4 Accounting and Finance; if you are in personnel management choose Profile C8 Personnel and Employee Relations.

- If you are a young manager at the outset of your career you may wish to leave it at that.

- If you are a little further ahead with your career you may wish to add one or two of the more general areas which are:

    C1 General Management

    C2 Business Policy

    C3 Organising and Dealing with People

- You may also wish to explore another functional area which you believe may be of particular importance to your career.

- Do not do more than three of the Functional Management Skills Profiles.

Remember you can, if you wish, at a later stage in working through this book, or at a later stage in your career go back and complete further Functional Management Skills Profiles. Certainly your skills will change over time, either improving or declining, and at later stages in your career you will need to re-do the skills profiles.

COUNSELLOR ADVICE

At this stage you would be wise to ask your counsellor to look through all the profiles you have completed to form a view of the reasonableness of your self-scoring on all the factors.

◀ SECTION 3
PRESENT POSITION PROFILE ▶

◀ SECTION 3

◀ PRESENT POSITION PROFILE ▶

You have so far analysed your views of your:

- Career and Performance Profile
- Personal Profile
- Personal Management Skills Profile
- Overall Management Skills Profile
- Functional Management Skills Profiles

It is now helpful for you to summarise your views on those profiles. Please proceed as follows.

CAREER AND PERFORMANCE PROFILE

- Read again through all your responses to the Career and Performance Profile.
- Amend them or expand them as necessary.
- Write a narrative summarising your view on your Career and Performance Profile.

EXAMPLE ▶ An example may be helpful. We have based this on a 27-year-old Chartered Accountant.

'I am a 27-year-old Chartered Accountant educated at an independent grammar school, followed by a degree in Management Sciences. I qualified as a Chartered Accountant after three years with a "big six" accounting firm passing all my examinations at the first attempt.

I attended all the relevant training courses to qualify as a Chartered Accountant. After qualifying I attended the long computer course and then worked as a Computer Audit Manager.

I left the "big six" firm to become firstly Assistant Company Secretary, then Assistant Financial Controller of a PLC with a turnover of around £300 million.

In that post my key objectives have been to settle into the post and become proficient at it, and to work actively on the integration into the PLC of a number of companies recently acquired. I believe that those objectives have been well met. In general I think I have performed well in that post with no specific areas of strength or weakness relevant to meeting those objectives.

My main strengths are a capacity for hard work, steadiness under extreme pressure, an ability to work successfully with superiors, peers, and subordinates, and a high level of organising ability. My main personal weakness is a tendency to overconscientiousness and working very long hours, though I am not a worrier.

The next job I would like is a Financial Director in one of our major subsidiaries. In my view, to prepare for that and for future progression my main requirement is the continued acquisition of experience on the lines available in my present post. I would prefer to remain in my present geographical area though that is not a major consideration to me.

I have taken steps to develop my career by acquiring outside my work, a wide familiarity with business issues and a familiarity with the use of business policy planning techniques.'

Having written your narrative, read it through carefully, compare it with your response to the Present Position Profile pro forma, and amend your narrative as appropriate.

PERSONAL PROFILE

- Read through your responses to the Personal Profile pro forma.
- Examine carefully your Personal Profile Summary and the comparison with the preferred scores for managers.
- Write yourself a narrative summarising your own view of your Personal Profile.

Again an example may be helpful, again based on the same 27-year-old Chartered Accountant.

◄ EXAMPLE

> 'I am a decisive person, though sometimes I tend to take decisions a little ahead of the facts. I am very determined, but show high levels of diplomacy in dealing with people.
>
> I have a great deal of drive, energy, and enthusiasm. My enthusiasm can sometimes lead me to an over-optimistic view of the prospects of success in a course of action I am interested in. I am fair-minded with people, and show flexibility in my dealings with others though not to the point of lack of purpose.
>
> I do seem to have a strongly marked ability to look forward and also regard myself as scrupulously honest, both socially and intellectually. I am intelligent and my judgement seems to be pretty good, though with a concern about over-decisiveness as mentioned above in the first paragraph.
>
> I am loyal to my subordinates, peers, and bosses though usually, I think, careful not to let this go so far as uncritical loyalty. I am highly reliable with, I think, a rather over-developed conscientiousness if that is possible. I am resilient under stressful circumstances and self-confident, though not always as confident as I appear.
>
> I have considerable self-control and rarely show aggravation. I am very stable and steady although calm is a word I would not choose to describe myself.'

Again, having written your narrative, read it through carefully and compare it with your responses to the Personal Profile pro forma, your Personal Profile Summary and the analysis of

preferred scores for managers. Amend or expand your narrative as appropriate.

PERSONAL MANAGEMENT SKILLS PROFILE

- Look at your responses to the Personal Management Skills Profile.
- Form a view on your five most significant skill strengths.
- Form a view on your five most significant skill weaknesses.
- List them as follows:

Personal Management Skills strengths

1. _____
2. _____
3. _____
4. _____
5. _____

Personal Management Skills weaknesses

1. _____
2. _____
3. _____
4. _____
5. _____

OVERALL MANAGEMENT SKILLS PROFILE

- Look at your responses to the Overall Management Skills profile.
- Form a view on your five most significant skill strengths.
- Form a view on your five most significant skill weaknesses.
- List them as follows:

Overall Management Skills strengths

1. _____
2. _____
3. _____
4. _____
5. _____

Overall Management Skills weaknesses

1. _____
2. _____
3. _____
4. _____
5. _____

FUNCTIONAL MANAGEMENT SKILLS PROFILES

For the Functional Management Skills Profiles you have completed:

- Look at your responses to each Functional Skills Profile.
- Form a view on your five most significant skills strengths.
- Form a view on your five most significant skills weaknesses.
- List them as shown below.
- You will recall that you were asked to choose one, two, or at the most three Functional Management Skills Profiles. The strengths and weaknesses schedule is therefore set out three times.

Profile title:
Functional Management Skills Profile strengths

1. _____

2. _____

3. _____

4. _____

5. _____

Functional Management Skills Profile weaknesses

1. _____
2. _____
3. _____
4. _____
5. _____

Profile title:
Functional Management Skills Profile strengths

1. _____
2. _____
3. _____
4. _____
5. _____

Functional Management Skills Profile weaknesses

1. _____
2. _____
3. _____
4. _____
5. _____

Profile title:
Functional Management Skills Profile strengths

1. _____
2. _____
3. _____
4. _____
5. _____

Functional Management Skills Profile weaknesses

1. _____
2. _____
3. _____
4. _____
5. _____

◀ SECTION 4
CAREER PLANNING GUIDE ▶

◀ SECTION 4

◀ CAREER PLANNING GUIDE ▶

INTRODUCTION

So far we have concentrated on your assessment of your present position. Now we shall look at your final career aspiration, at the likely programme of jobs you see as leading to that final aspiration, and at an assessment of your learning needs to enable you to move from where you are now to where you want to be, in your career.

Why should you bother to plan your career at all? The main reason is simply that if you do, you are much more likely to reach career success, however you personally define it, than if you do not.

You must, of course, be good at your present job and seek to improve your performance in it. However, simply doing that and waiting for opportunities to arise is not a sensible career strategy. You have to be good at both your job and at managing your career.

Throughout your career you will find that your track record or Curriculum Vitae is of crucial importance to further career achievement. Therefore your track record is one of your major assets and needs to be tended and developed as such. Acquiring a track record which you can market successfully needs to be one of your main concerns and will require care and effort throughout your career.

Looking into the future is obviously both difficult and inaccurate. Nevertheless you will need to make the attempt as suggested in this section if you are to improve your career prospects. We should emphasise that none of your answers on the various issues can possibly be complete, nor are they likely to be accurate. Also you are almost certain to change your views over time and will therefore need to repeat the whole exercise regularly, preferably at annual intervals.

An obvious place to start your career planning would be with your present post. However, as the old joke has it 'If I were you I would not start from here'. You have already, in earlier sections, set down many points about your present post. Now it is wise to raise your eyes to the distant future before returning to the present and then to an action plan.

YOUR FINAL POST

What we are saying is that the time horizon you should consider is not two years, five years, or ten years, but your complete career. The basic outline of your career needs to be considered early on so that it can be shaped by you.

The following points are relevant in considering the post you see as your final career aspiration.

- Try to be creative and not become too obsessed with a narrow view based on your present limitations.

- Try to generate a number of alternative options. The options can be as many as you like but it is possibly wise to limit them to five.

- Each option needs to be detailed, not simply broad or ill-defined.

- Then evaluate each of the options carefully in terms of

    — aspects which attract you;

    — aspects which seem to be disadvantages;

- — constraints on your choice;
- — whether you really are prepared to seek to achieve that goal.
- In making your evaluation you need to examine the assumptions about the outside environment which you have built into your thinking and question whether those assumptions are likely to be valid.
- In making your choice you need to strike a balance between over-optimism and realism.
- Finally, write a short description of your final career aspiration post, read it through carefully, amend it as necessary, then settle on your final version.

SKILLS ANALYSIS

What we now want to do is form a view on the level of skills required in the final post you have chosen.

- You may well feel able to form that view yourself. If not, consult your counsellor or indeed any other experienced manager whose view you think may be valuable.
- We need to evaluate the final post skills using a number of the skills profiles we have already used earlier in this book and which appear in Section 6.
- If your final post aspiration is a general management post then simply use Profile A - Personal Management Skills, and Profile B - Overall Management Skills.
- If your final post aspiration is a 'head of function' post, then in addition to Profiles A and B complete the relevant Functional Management Skills Profile.

For each profile you are completing proceed as follows:

- Enter in red onto the relevant profile in Section 6 the level of skill you believe to be required in your final post aspiration.

- You will already have on the various profiles your own view on your present skill level on each factor.

- Form a preliminary view on the gaps between the skill level necessary for your final post aspiration and the level you have now.

- A problem you will have is that there will be many sizeable gaps, and all of them will be important.

- Obviously all the gaps must be borne in mind.

KEY GAPS

However, you have no possibility of remedying all these gaps quickly. It is therefore wise, for each of the skills profiles you have completed with respect to your final career aspiration, to pick out the ten most significant gaps, ie those which seem to you to be biggest and/or most important.

Personal Skills Profile gaps

1. _____
2. _____
3. _____
4. _____
5. _____
6. _____
7. _____
8. _____
9. _____
10. _____

Overall Skills Profile gaps

1. _____
2. _____
3. _____
4. _____
5. _____
6. _____
7. _____
8. _____
9. _____
10. _____

Functional Management Skills Profile gaps

1. _____
2. _____
3. _____
4. _____
5. _____
6. _____
7. _____
8. _____
9. _____
10. _____

GAPS SUMMARY

You now have an overall summary of what you see as your key skill gaps in reaching your final career aspiration. Remember you are recommended to repeat the analysis annually so there will be plenty of opportunity to change your view over time.

Later we shall look at building an action programme to fill these gaps and to further your career. However, before we do that we need to give thought to how you see your progression towards your final post. Again your views will not be accurate and will certainly be subject to change.

JOB PROGRESSION

Over the next two pages (pages 67 and 68) you will see a Job Progression Analysis. Please complete it as follows:

- You are unlikely to be able to see, even inaccurately, beyond seven jobs. The Job Progression Analysis is therefore confined to seven.

- Enter under *Job 7* a short description of your final career aspiration post, ie title, organisation size, broad duties and also the rough time when you would expect to achieve it, remembering that you have already given a lot of thought to this post.

- Now enter similar information about your present post.

- Now enter similar information for the other posts you feel you can foresee on the way to your final post.

An example may be helpful, keeping the summary of each job to a minimum for illustration purposes. The example is based on the young Chartered Accountant we used as an example in Section 3, but based on the time when he was still an Audit Senior.

Job 1 (present)
Audit senior, major accounting firm.

◀ EXAMPLE

Job 2
Audit manager, major accounting firm.

Job 3
Accountant, medium-sized company (say) £20m to £30m turnover.

Job 4
Financial controller, medium-sized company (say) £20m to £30m turnover.

Job 5
Financial director, medium-sized company (say) £20m to £30m turnover.

Job 6
Financial director, larger company (say) £50m to £100m turnover.

Job 7
Managing director of company of (say) £50m to £100m turnover.

You will no doubt realise, if you turn back to page 50 that when he wrote his Career and Performance Profile this young manager was already occupying *Job 3* on his Job Progression Analysis. You will also realise that already his career has not precisely followed the pattern he predicted when as an audit senior he compiled his Job Progression Analysis.

That obviously is entirely normal and it would be naive to expect otherwise. This is why we recommend on page 64 that you review your aspirations and plans regularly, preferably at annual intervals.

JOB PROGRESSION ANALYSIS ▶

Job 1

Date now

Present job title and outline job summary

Possible future job titles and outline job summaries

Job 2

| approximate date |

Job 3

| approximate date |

Job 4

| approximate date |

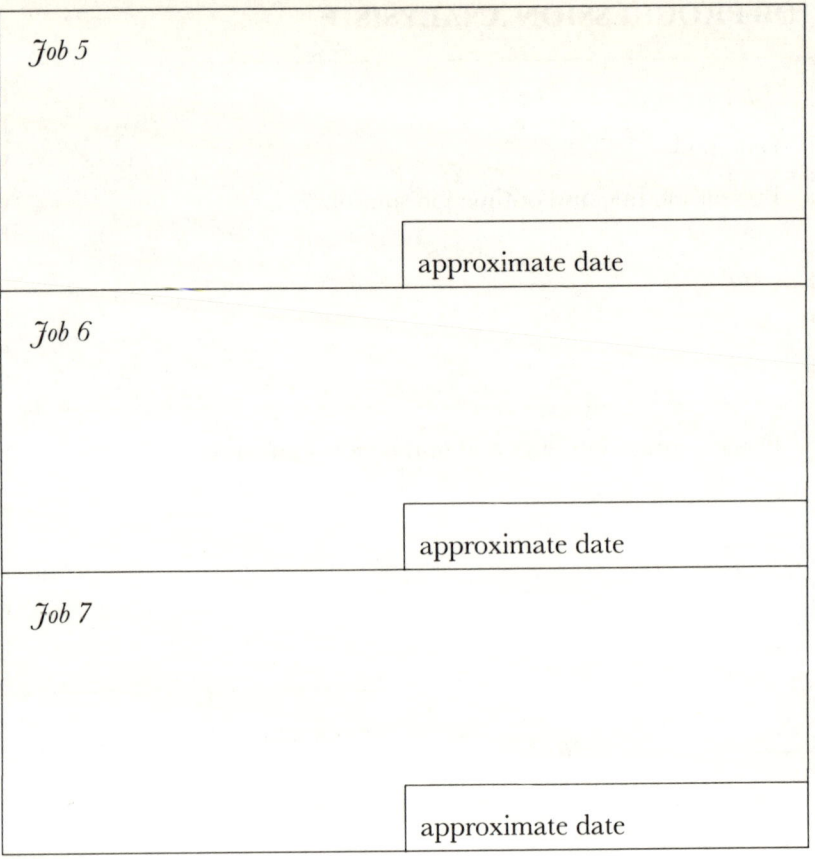

SKILLS PROGRESSION

Now we want to look at the sort of progression in filling your skills gaps that may be appropriate.

It is usually better to confine that analysis to the ten most significant gaps under each of the relevant skills profiles. On the following schedule simply tick the time in your career when you feel that the relevant skill gap must be filled. Again this will inevitably be tentative and subject to later revision.

Personal Skills Profile gaps

Title	Job 1	Job 2	Job 3	Job 4	Job 5	Job 6	Job 7
1.							
2.							
3.							
4.							
5.							
6.							
7.							
8.							
9.							
10.							

Overall Skills Profile gaps

Title	Job 1	Job 2	Job 3	Job 4	Job 5	Job 6	Job 7
1.							
2.							
3.							
4.							
5.							
6.							
7.							
8.							
9.							
10.							

Functional Management Skills Profile gaps

Title	Job 1	Job 2	Job 3	Job 4	Job 5	Job 6	Job 7
1.							
2.							
3.							
4.							
5.							
6.							
7.							
8.							
9.							
10.							

IMPROVING YOUR SKILLS

This book is not a manual of management development opportunities or techniques. However, it should be emphasised that

- you yourself have the key role in improving your skills. Your organisation may well be willing to help but you cannot rely on that, you must be prepared to take the initiative. You would be wise to consult your counsellor again at this stage;
- you need to make yourself aware of the facilities and techniques which are available.

The main approaches to the development of management skills are:

- *learning by doing* – simply 'having a go' possibly under controlled conditions but very probably not, and acquiring skill by doing so.
- *learning by example* – observing a skilled practitioner and seeking to emulate that practitioner.
- *structured instruction on the job* – a carefully considered programme of instruction carried out on the job.
- *coaching* – an extension of structured instruction where a coach has very close involvement.
- *internal courses* – a planned course of instruction, using a range of methods, held within the organisation.
- *external courses* (including night school and day release) – a planned course of instruction using a range of methods, held outside the organisation.
- *distance learning* – a structured learning method involving closely programmed texts, with audio, video, and possibly interactive computerised techniques.
- *correspondence courses* – structured learning by correspondence.
- *personal study* – the manager simply learns by following a personally organised or externally organised programme of reading and skill development.
- *group learning* – any form of learning which is carried out in an interactive group rather than as individuals.
- *management games* – a structured learning method involving the simulation of competing and interacting companies in an artificially changing environment.
- *case studies* – an account of a management situation drawn from real life which a group of managers can study and use as a vehicle for planned learning.

- *case histories* – an account of a management situation drawn from real life with general comments but not used as a vehicle for group learning.
- *action learning* – learning through a series of projects and by doing real work rather than studying in a classroom although some classroom teaching may be involved.
- *qualifying courses* – there is a wide range of qualifying courses in management run by universities, polytechnics and other educational establishments, or by one of the professional bodies. They make varying levels of demand both intellectually and in time commitment.

To put it very simply:

- Become familiar with each of these approaches.
- Become familiar with current sources of those approaches.
- Continually examine your skill gaps.
- Continually seek the appropriate approach to filling your skill gaps.

ACTION PLANNING: YOUR NEXT MOVE

Having looked forward to your final post aspiration, and looked at various possible posts progressing towards that, the first thing you should now do is to concentrate again on your next job.

- Again, what do you want your next job to be?
- Do you think it will be inside or outside your current organisation?
- Are such jobs available now?
- Are you, or will you shortly be, really qualified for such a job?
- If not, is the prospect realistic?

- If it is not realistic, what will you do?
  — Change your next job aspiration?
  — Change your qualifications and skills and wait?
- How do such jobs become available?
- How are you going to plan to move towards such a job?
- What are the main difficulties in moving?

  1. _____
  2. _____
  3. _____
  4. _____
  5. _____

- What further steps are you now going to take to enable you to move?

  1. _____
  2. _____
  3. _____
  4. _____
  5. _____

ACTION PLANNING: LONGER TERM

You have already taken three steps in action planning:

1. Forecast your job progression.
2. Analysed your skill gaps and looked at how to fill them.
3. Planned your next job move.

Your key planning tool is your Job Progression Analysis. As you move through your career you will need to plan each step in a similar fashion to that already discussed for your next job. However, a number of general issues are relevant.

- Learning can be very difficult when you are filling a demanding job. There really is no simple answer to that, you need to be aware of the balance. A job which after, say, one year in post does not leave some freedom for learning is probably unsuitable for you.

- Up to the age of 30 the key considerations are acquiring skills, qualifications and experience. Salary, while important, should not become the most important issue.

- No career is a faultless upward progress. You may well encounter setbacks. A difficult boss, a takeover, a failure on your part to meet the needs of a job. You need to accept that such setbacks can occur and be prepared to re-cast your career plan if necessary.

- Learning to sell yourself and having the right image are instrumental to career success, though you need to be careful not to overdo it.

Suggested approaches to selling yourself are:

- Analyse the industry and your company. Be pro-establishment. If you cannot broadly accept the basic values of your organisation you are in the wrong place.

- Be helpful to superiors, peers and subordinates.

- Make sure that colleagues know of your success.

- Find ways to stand out from your peers and get known to your superiors.

- Get a reputation for getting things done.

- Stay steady. You will be judged adversely for one example of rash or panicky behaviour while countless other instances of strength may be ignored.

- Demonstrate complete reliability.
- Learn to make a good presentation using all the relevant techniques.
- Build a strong team which complements your skills.
- Carefully nurture your business friends and contacts.
- Never deprecate your colleagues.

An unexpected opportunity may occur. Do not regard your career plan as so rigid that you do not consider taking advantage of such an opportunity.

◀ SECTION 5　CONCLUSION ▶

◀ SECTION 5

◀ CONCLUSION ▶

This book has sought to help you with self-assessment, leading to developing yourself towards greater career success.

At the risk of being repetitive, a few concluding points may be useful.

SUCCESS

Success is defined by you, not by the authors and not by anybody else.

CHANGING VIEWS

You may, indeed almost certainly will, change your view about success over time. It is rare for a view of success found at the start of a career to remain intact throughout that career.

SELF-DEVELOPMENT

Career development is self-development. You may get help from your employer or from others, but your development is really a matter for you.

CONTINUOUS DEVELOPMENT

Your development is continuous throughout your career and takes place in a subtly changing context of your views, your opportunities, and the development experiences open to you.

CAREER CHOICE

Career choice is a process, not an event, and again is continuous throughout your career. What the system outlined in this book seeks to do is to help you with that choice at one particular time in your career. It is assumed that you will then repeat the process at regular intervals, preferably annually, emphasising the continuous nature of the career choice process.

A COUNSELLOR

You are recommended to find yourself a suitably experienced counsellor or mentor to give you an outside judgement of you and your career analysis. Such a person can be invaluable to you. Again, of course, you may require a different counsellor at different stages of your career and with varying degrees of formality or informality in your relationship.

CAREER AND PERFORMANCE PROFILE

You have been encouraged to look searchingly at your career to date and to analyse your performance critically.

PERSONAL PROFILE

You have been encouraged to look searchingly at your personality and to form a view on the suitability of that personality for a management career.

SKILLS PROFILES

You have been encouraged to look searchingly at your levels of skills in various areas, not vaguely and in broad terms, but in highly specific and concrete terms.

CAREER PLANNING

You have been encouraged to make a coherent attempt to form a plan for your whole career, again on the assumption that you will revise that plan at annual intervals.

SKILL DEVELOPMENT

You have been encouraged to analyse the gaps in your skills which are relevant now and which are relevant to your long-term career aspirations.

ACTION PLAN

You have also been encouraged to form an action plan to fill those skills gaps at appropriate times in your career.

It remains only for the authors to wish you luck in your career, and success, however you decide to define it.

◀ SECTION 6   APPENDICES ▶

◀ SECTION 6

◀ APPENDICES ▶

MANAGEMENT SKILLS PROFILE QUESTIONNAIRES

This section contains the full set of Management Skills Profile Questionnaires as follows:

Profile A	–	Personal Management Skills Profile
Profile B	–	Overall Management Skills Profile
Profile C1	–	General Management
Profile C2	–	Business Policy
Profile C3	–	Organising and Dealing with People
Profile C4	–	Accounting and Finance
Profile C5	–	Operations
Profile C6	–	Marketing and Sales
Profile C7	–	Research and Product Development
Profile C8	–	Personnel and Employee Relations
Profile C9	–	Purchasing
Profile C10	–	Exporting
Profile C11	–	Information Technology
Profile C12	–	New Technology
Profile C13	–	Retailing, Warehousing and Distribution

PROFILE A
PERSONAL MANAGEMENT SKILLS PROFILE ▶
SELF-ASSESSMENT QUESTIONNAIRE

Preamble

Listed below is a range of the personal management skills which are relevant to a wide range of management appointments. None of us have all these skills and our skill levels vary considerably across the range and over time.

Please read the list and consider it. Then tick the level of skill you feel that you have at present in each area.

One would expect a capable and experienced senior manager to have varying levels of skills depending on that manager's organisation level, specialisation, past training and experience.

The broad comparison you are asked to make is with the personal management skills you think would be needed as, say,

- A Chief Executive of a medium-sized business of, say, £20m to £30m turnover, or around 1,000 employees;

- a unit general manager in the NHS, for example, a Hospital General Manager;

- a Chief Executive of a District Council of, say, 100,000 population.

One would expect occupants of these jobs to score themselves 'Good' or higher on a high proportion of the skills.

There is inevitably some overlap in the areas and room for some difference of view about definitions. The objective is to arrive at a reasonable overall self-assessment for your own use.

As you will see, the skill levels are categorised as follows:

None No significant level of skill and/or knowledge.

Some Some knowledge and/or skill but lower than you would prefer.

Reasonable Reasonable level of knowledge and/or skill enabling you to cope in that area without major difficulties.

Good   Good level of knowledge and/or skill enabling you to cope more adequately. Probably about average for a senior manager in a medium-sized business.

High   High skill and/or knowledge level such as to encourage you to feel rather pleased with your performance.

Very high   Very high skill and/or knowledge level. You regard yourself as outstanding and your colleagues sometimes comment favourably.

The skill areas are listed alphabetically.

	None	Some	Reasonable	Good	High	Very high
1. Appraisal of subordinates						
2. Attention to detail						
3. Coaching of subordinates						
4. Communication skills – general						
5. Comprehension and analysis of facts and figures						
6. Confidence in dealing with subordinates, peers and superiors						
7. Creation of original ideas						
8. Decision-making style						
9. Delegation to, and control of, subordinates						
10. Discipline – self						
11. Discipline – subordinates						

PERSONAL MANAGEMENT SKILLS PROFILE ▶ 89

	None	Some	Reasonable	Good	High	Very high
12. Effectiveness in getting things done						
13. Information system – personal – creation and use						
14. Interviewing skills						
15. Judgement of people and situations						
16. Leadership style						
17. Meetings – chairmanship						
18. Meetings – participation						
19. Negotiating skills						
20. Objective setting – self						
21. Objective setting – subordinates						
22. Personal paperwork control – desk control						

	None	Some	Reasonable	Good	High	Very high
23. *Personal impact – appearance, style*						
24. *Personal impact – speech*						
25. *Reading skills – speed and comprehension*						
26. *Report writing*						
27. *Selection of subordinates*						
28. *Selling skills*						
29. *Telephone skills*						
30. *Time management – personal*						
31. *Secretarial assistance – use and control*						
32. *Verbal presentations*						
33. *Languages* Language _____ Language _____						

PROFILE B
OVERALL MANAGEMENT SKILLS PROFILE ▶
SELF-ASSESSMENT QUESTIONNAIRE

Preamble

Listed below is a range of overall management skills covering the major areas of skill and knowledge required in the overall management of an organisation. As with the Personal Skills Profile none of us have all these skills and our skill levels vary considerably across the range and over time.

Please read the list and consider it. Then ring the level of skill you feel that you have at present in each area. Obviously the skill levels needed to run, say, a small garage, are different from those needed to run ICI, so you need a basis of comparison. The broad comparison you are asked to make is with the skills you think are needed as, say,

- a Chief Executive of a medium-sized business of, say, £20m to £30m turnover or around 1,000 employees;
- a unit general manager in the NHS, for example, a Hospital General Manager;
- a Chief Executive of a District Council of, say, 100,000 population.

One would expect a capable and experienced senior manager to have a varying level of these skills depending on the person's managerial level, specialisation and past training and experience.

As examples:

1. A managing director would be likely to feel that business policy and general management skills are at the least 'Reasonable', and probably 'Good' or higher.

2. An accountant still working in the accounting and finance area would probably expect to have accounting and finance skills rated 'High'. However, if the accountant has moved to a different role in another function or at general manager level,

the accounting and finance knowledge and skills would probably be regarded as being somewhat lower than that.

There is inevitably some overlap in the areas and room for some difference of view about definitions. The objective is to arrive at a reasonable overall self-assessment for your own use.

The areas are not listed alphabetically nor in order of importance, except possibly for General Management and Business Policy.

The ratings are as follows:

None　　　　No significant level of skill and/or knowledge.

Some　　　　Some knowledge and/or skill but lower than you would prefer.

Reasonable　Reasonable level of knowledge and/or skill enabling you to cope in that area without major difficulties.

Good　　　　Good level of knowledge and/or skill enabling you to cope more than adequately. Probably about average for a senior manager in a medium-sized business.

High　　　　High skill and/or knowledge level such as to encourage you to feel rather pleased with your performance.

Very high　Very high skill and/or knowledge level. You regard yourself as outstanding and your colleagues sometimes comment favourably.

OVERALL MANAGEMENT SKILLS PROFILE ▶ 93

1. *General management*
   Ability to carry through the business policy plan, manage the overall business in the short, medium, and long term, paying adequate attention to the major functions.

   None   Some   Reasonable   Good   High   Very high

2. *Business policy*
   Ability to put together soundly based and documented business policy plans for a medium-sized organisation having considered and documented a number of alternative options in some detail.

   None   Some   Reasonable   Good   High   Very high

3. *Organising and dealing with people*
   Ability to achieve results through people, preserving a balance between short, medium, and long-term goals of the business, and the need to retain staff morale and commitment.

   None   Some   Reasonable   Good   High   Very high

4. *Accounting and finance*
   Ability to understand and manage the main accounting and finance issues in a medium-sized organisation.

   None   Some   Reasonable   Good   High   Very high

5. *Operations*
   Ability to manage the operational function for goods or services in your organisation's area of activity, with a broad appreciation of overall efficiency.

   It is important to realise that the term 'operations' is not specific to a particular sector. It means making cars in the car industry, building houses in the building industry, providing service in a hospital, processing chemicals in the chemical industry, etc.

   None   Some   Reasonable   Good   High   Very high

6. *Marketing and sales*
   Ability to analyse the market, develop marketing plans, organise the sales function, and achieve satisfactory sales performance in your own organisation's area of activity.

   None   Some   Reasonable   Good   High   Very high

7. *Research and product development*
   Ability to manage basic research in areas likely to be relevant to your organisation and/or the ability to manage the initiation and development of new products from the conceptual stage to manufacture in your organisation's area of activity.

   None   Some   Reasonable   Good   High   Very high

8. *Personnel and employee relations*
   Ability to develop personnel and industrial relations policies and to manage those policies in the short, medium, and long term.

   None   Some   Reasonable   Good   High   Very high

9. *Purchasing*
   Management of the purchasing function, including the sourcing of materials and components from the home market and overseas to optimum economic effectiveness to meet the organisation's needs in its broad areas of business.

   None   Some   Reasonable   Good   High   Very high

10. *Exporting*
    Management of the penetration of existing and potential export markets in your organisation's business area, including marketing, selling, and administration.

    None   Some   Reasonable   Good   High   Very high

11. *Information technology*
    Management of information technology arrangements suitable for your company's needs both with regard to existing facilities and also to facilities to meet its developing requirements.

    None   Some   Reasonable   Good   High   Very high

12. *New technology*
    Knowledge and appreciation of the emerging new technology relevant to your organisation's business area.

    None   Some   Reasonable   Good   High   Very high

13. *Retailing, warehousing and distribution*
    Management of activities required to organise the efficient movement and storage of incoming materials and finished products, and the variety of means available to ensure the most effective distribution of finished products to customers and consumers.

    None   Some   Reasonable   Good   High   Very high

Other Areas
Define your skill and knowledge level in any other relevant areas not covered above.

   Area 1 _____

   None   Some   Reasonable   Good   High   Very high

   Area 2 _____

   None   Some   Reasonable   Good   High   Very high

FUNCTIONAL SKILLS PROFILE C1
GENERAL MANAGEMENT ▶

Preamble

Listed below is a range of the skills involved in general management.

We define general management as the ability to carry through the business policy plan and manage the overall business in the short, medium, and long term, paying adequate attention to the major functions.

Please read the list and consider it. Then ring the level of skill you feel that you have at present in each area. The broad comparison is with the skills needed as, say,

- a Chief Executive of a medium-sized business of, say, £20m to £30m turnover or around 1,000 employees;
- a unit general manager in the NHS, for example, a Hospital General Manager;
- a Chief Executive of a District Council of, say, 100,000 population.

One would expect a capable and experienced senior manager to have a varying level of these skills depending on managerial level, specialisation, past training, and experience. There is inevitably some overlap in many of the areas and room for some difference of view about definitions. The objective is to arrive at a reasonable overall self-assessment for your own use.

The ratings are as follows:

None No significant level of skill and/or knowledge.

Some Some knowledge and/or skill but lower than you would prefer.

Reasonable Reasonable level of knowledge and/or skill enabling you to cope in that area without major difficulties.

Good Good level of knowledge and/or skill enabling you to cope more than adequately. Probably about average for a senior manager in a medium-sized business.

High   High skill and/or knowledge level such as to feel rather pleased with your performance.

Very high   Very high skill and/or knowledge level. You regard yourself as outstanding and your colleagues sometimes comment favourably.

The areas are subdivided and are not listed in order of importance.

General

General management involves the use of a wide range of skills. The key skill areas are those covered in the Overall Management Skills Profile which you should already have completed; if not, please do so. Those skills are:

General management	This Profile
Business policy	Profile C2
Organising and dealing with people	Profile C3
Accounting and finance	Profile C4
Operations	Profile C5
Marketing and sales	Profile C6
Research and product development	Profile C7
Personnel and employee relations	Profile C8
Purchasing	Profile C9
Exporting	Profile C10
Information technology	Profile C11
New technology	Profile C12
Retailing, warehousing and distribution	Profile C13

Having completed the Overall Management Skills Profile, you should now complete some detailed skill profiles from the above list which are specifically relevant to your business and situation as described in the text under the heading 'Competence Review – Functional Management Skills Profiles' on page 45.

However, in this present Profile C1 General Management, we will also consider some extra skills which do not specifically appear either in the Personal Skills Profile, the Overall Management Skills Profile, or in Profiles C2 to C13. These extra skills are shown below and you should now complete those items of Profile C1.

People

People management skills; one to one; in small groups; in large groups.

1. *Leadership style*
   Awareness of leadership style and an ability to operate a style appropriate to differing circumstances.

   None   Some   Reasonable   Good   High   Very high

2. *Delegation*
   Understanding of the principles of delegation and the ability to delegate appropriately.

   None   Some   Reasonable   Good   High   Very high

3. *Managing managers*
   Ability to manage and motivate subordinates who are themselves managing others.

   None   Some   Reasonable   Good   High   Very high

4. *Managing objectives*
   Ability to set appropriate objectives for subordinates and manage the achievement of those objectives.

   None   Some   Reasonable   Good   High   Very high

5. *Appraisal*
   Ability to appraise managers and staff at appropriate intervals in a way which encourages high performance.

   None   Some   Reasonable   Good   High   Very high

6. *Control of devolved managers*
   Ability to control managers devolved at outlying locations including overseas locations, in a way which encourages high performance.

   None   Some   Reasonable   Good   High   Very high

7. *Manager development*
   Ability to manage the development of managers to ensure high motivation and steady development towards possible future roles.

   None   Some   Reasonable   Good   High   Very high

8. *Manage job satisfaction*
   Ability to manage in a way which encourages job satisfaction while encouraging high performance.

   None   Some   Reasonable   Good   High   Very high

9. *Recruitment of managers*
   Knowledge of the skills of management recruitment and the ability to use those skills to choose managers for business success.

   None   Some   Reasonable   Good   High   Very high

Organisation

10. *Organisation structure and design*
    Awareness of different types of organisation structure, the ability to design suitable structures and adjust them to meet changing business needs.

    None   Some   Reasonable   Good   High   Very high

11. *Groups*
    Awareness of the organisation of committees, teams, project teams, and working groups of all kinds, and the ability to create and use such groups effectively.

    None   Some   Reasonable   Good   High   Very high

12. *Job design*
    Awareness of the principles of job design and the ability to design and re-design jobs to encourage high performance.

    None   Some   Reasonable   Good   High   Very high

External relations

13. Ability to manage external relations with shareholders to the advantage of the business.

    None   Some   Reasonable   Good   High   Very high

14. Ability to manage external relations with city opinion to the advantage of the business.

    None   Some   Reasonable   Good   High   Very high

15. Ability to manage external relations with public opinion to the advantage of the business.

    None   Some   Reasonable   Good   High   Very high

16. Ability to manage external relations with government agencies to the advantage of the business.

    None   Some   Reasonable   Good   High   Very high

GENERAL MANAGEMENT ▶ 101

Policy

17. Ability to manage an acquisitions programme.

    None   Some   Reasonable   Good   High   Very high

18. Ability to manage a divestment programme.

    None   Some   Reasonable   Good   High   Very high

19. Ability to manage a period of rapid internally-generated expansion.

    None   Some   Reasonable   Good   High   Very high

20. Ability to manage a period of rapid contraction.

    None   Some   Reasonable   Good   High   Very high

21. Ability to manage the opportunities and risks of overseas operations.

    None   Some   Reasonable   Good   High   Very high

22. Ability to manage the business opportunities and risks of currency fluctuations.

    None   Some   Reasonable   Good   High   Very high

23. Appreciation of the factors relevant to financial collapse and the ability to manage so as to minimise the risks of collapse.

    None   Some   Reasonable   Good   High   Very high

Board Operation

A knowledge of the key issues in the operation of boards of directors of companies.

---

24. *Board types*
Holding companies, private companies, listed public companies, USM companies, divisional boards, subsidiary boards, management boards.

None   Some   Reasonable   Good   High   Very high

---

25. *Board responsibilities*
Knowledge of the responsibilities of a board to shareholders, employees, customers, suppliers and the law.

None   Some   Reasonable   Good   High   Very high

---

26. *Board membership*
Membership issues including chairmanship, executive directors, non-executive directors.

None   Some   Reasonable   Good   High   Very high

---

27. *Board meetings*
Knowledge of the usual frequency, agendas, papers, committees, minutes, routines and behaviour patterns of board meetings.

None   Some   Reasonable   Good   High   Very high

---

28. *Board procedure*
Ability to manage the business within the broad framework implicit in this section.

None   Some   Reasonable   Good   High   Very high

Budget and Action Plan Management

29. *Budgets*
    Ability to manage using budgeted trading statements, balance sheets and cash flow statements to achieve results.

    None   Some   Reasonable   Good   High   Very high

30. *Trading statements*
    Ability to manage using budgets for sales, direct expense, gross margins, overhead and profit; on a monthly, quarterly, half annual and annual basis.

    None   Some   Reasonable   Good   High   Very high

31. *Action plans*
    Ability to manage using a detailed action plan orientated to meet business objectives.

    None   Some   Reasonable   Good   High   Very high

Techniques

32. *Critical paths*
    Knowledge of the evaluation of critical paths in projects and the ability to manage using those critical path assessments.

    None   Some   Reasonable   Good   High   Very high

33. *Flow charts*
    Knowledge of flow charting and the ability to manage using flow charts.

    None   Some   Reasonable   Good   High   Very high

34. *Decision trees*
    Knowledge of decision trees and the ability to manage using that knowledge.

    None   Some   Reasonable   Good   High   Very high

35. *Project management*
    Overall awareness of project management skills and the ability to manage discrete projects.

    None   Some   Reasonable   Good   High   Very high

36. *Profit improvement*
    Knowledge of profit improvement techniques and the ability to improve profit using them.

    None   Some   Reasonable   Good   High   Very high

37. *Managing change*
    Knowledge of the issues and techniques involved in managing change and the ability to manage change successfully.

    None   Some   Reasonable   Good   High   Very high

38. *Contingency plans*
    Knowledge of contingency planning techniques and the ability to use them.

    None   Some   Reasonable   Good   High   Very high

39. *Information systems*
    Ability to manage the business successfully using the management information systems and to modify those systems as necessary.

    None   Some   Reasonable   Good   High   Very high

40. *Communication*

Knowledge of communication techniques and issues within the business and the ability to use them for improved performance.

None   Some   Reasonable   Good   High   Very high

FUNCTIONAL SKILLS PROFILE C2
BUSINESS POLICY ▶

Preamble

Listed below is a range of the skills involved in managing business policy.

We define the management of business policy generally as the ability to put together soundly based and documented business policy plans for a medium-sized organisation having considered and documented a number of alternative options in some detail; the final documentation to cover all the functions set out in the Overall Management Skills Profile.

Please read the list and consider it. Then ring or tick the level of skill you feel that you have at present in each area. The broad comparison is with the skills needed as, say,

- a Chief Executive of a medium-sized business of, say, £20m to £30m turnover or around 1,000 employees;

- a unit general manager in the NHS, for example, a Hospital General Manager;

- a Chief Executive of a District Council of, say, 100,000 population.

One would expect a capable and experienced senior manager to have a varying level of these skills depending on managerial level, specialisation, past training, and experience.

There is inevitably some overlap in many of the areas and room for some difference of view about definitions. The objective is to arrive at a reasonable overall self-assessment for your own use.

The ratings are as follows:

None   No significant level of skill and/or knowledge.

Some   Some knowledge and/or skill but lower than you would prefer.

Reasonable Reasonable level of knowledge and/or skill enabling you to cope in that area without major difficulties.

Good   Good level of knowledge and/or skill enabling you to cope more than adequately. Probably about average for a senior manager in a medium-sized business.

High   High skill and/or knowledge level such as to encourage you to feel rather pleased with your performance.

Very high   Very high skill and/or knowledge level. You regard yourself as outstanding and your colleagues sometimes comment favourably.

The areas are subdivided and are not listed in order of importance.

Accounting and Finance

The necessary accounting and finance skills for considering and documenting business policy plans. There are a wide range of these and the following are particularly important.

---

1. *Financial structure*
   Knowledge of the various types and sources of finance used.

   None   Some   Reasonable   Good   High   Very high

---

2. *Trading statements*
   Knowledge of the creation and interpretation of trading statements.

   None   Some   Reasonable   Good   High   Very high

---

3. *Balance sheets*
   Knowledge of the creation and interpretation of balance sheets.

   None   Some   Reasonable   Good   High   Very high

4. *Cash flow*
   Knowledge of the creation and interpretation of cash flow statements and cash flow forecasts.

   None   Some   Reasonable   Good   High   Very high

5. *Tax*
   Outline knowledge of major tax issues.

   None   Some   Reasonable   Good   High   Very high

6. *Management accounts*
   Ability to interpret management accounts.

   None   Some   Reasonable   Good   High   Very high

7. *Costing*
   Outline knowledge of standard costing, process costing, contract costing, job costing, marginal and absorption costing.

   None   Some   Reasonable   Good   High   Very high

Behaviour Issues

8. Appreciation of the organisational behaviour issues likely to affect the business policy planning process and the achievement of planned results.

   None   Some   Reasonable   Good   High   Very high

Board Operation

A knowledge of the key issues in the operations of boards of directors of companies.

9. *Board types*
   Holding companies, private companies, listed public companies, USM companies, divisional boards, subsidiary boards, management boards.

   None   Some   Reasonable   Good   High   Very high

10. *Board responsibilities*
    Knowledge of the responsibilities of a board to shareholders, employees, customers, suppliers and the law.

    None   Some   Reasonable   Good   High   Very high

11. *Board membership*
    Membership issues including chairmanship, executive directors, non-executive directors.

    None   Some   Reasonable   Good   High   Very high

12. *Board meetings*
    Knowledge of the usual frequency, agendas, papers, committees, minutes, routines and behaviour patterns of board meetings.

    None   Some   Reasonable   Good   High   Very high

13. *Board procedure*
    Knowledge of board procedures, election of chairman, election of chief executive, appointment of executive and non-executive directors.

    None   Some   Reasonable   Good   High   Very high

Budgets and Budgeting

14. *General*
    Broad knowledge of the creation and interpretation of budgeted trading statements, balance sheets and cash flow statements.

    None   Some   Reasonable   Good   High   Very high

15. *Trading statements*
    Broad knowledge of budgeting for sales, direct expense, gross margins, overhead and profit; on a monthly, quarterly, half annual, and annual basis.

    None   Some   Reasonable   Good   High   Very high

Chief Executive

16. Overall appreciation of the role of the Chief Executive in the development, board discussion, management, and achievement of business policy plans.

    None   Some   Reasonable   Good   High   Very high

Culture

17. Defining company culture as its learned patterns of managerial and employee attitude, style and behaviour; a broad knowledge of the variations in culture and the problems of changing culture.

    None   Some   Reasonable   Good   High   Very high

Implementing and Updating Business Policy Plans and Budgets

18. *Action plans*
    Knowledge of the creation and use of business policy action plans and budgets (see budgets in more detail above).

    None   Some   Reasonable   Good   High   Very high

19. *Monitoring*
    Ability to organise and manage the monitoring of performance against agreed action plans and budgets.

    None   Some   Reasonable   Good   High   Very high

20. *Updating*
    Knowledge of the appropriate frequency and procedures for updating plans.

    None   Some   Reasonable   Good   High   Very high

Investigation and Appraisal of Proposed Developments

21. *Acquisitions*
    Ability to evaluate and report upon potential acquisitions.

    None   Some   Reasonable   Good   High   Very high

22. *Project evaluation*
    Ability to evaluate and report upon new business projects.

    None   Some   Reasonable   Good   High   Very high

23. *Capital expenditure appraisal*
    Ability to evaluate and report upon new capital projects.

    None   Some   Reasonable   Good   High   Very high

---

24. *Techniques*
    Knowledge of the techniques used in evaluating new projects (discounted cash flow, internal rate of return, payback period).

    None   Some   Reasonable   Good   High   Very high

Literature

There is a wide range of literature on the subject of business policy. What is your familiarity with the following?

---

25. Ansoff HI, *Business Strategy* (1969).

    None   Some   Reasonable   Good   High   Very high

---

26. Argenti J, *Practical Corporate Planning* (1989).

    None   Some   Reasonable   Good   High   Very high

---

27. Goldsmith, W and Clutterbuck, D, *The Winning Streak* (1984).

    None   Some   Reasonable   Good   High   Very high

---

28. Peters, T J and Waterman, RH, *In Search of Excellence* (1982).

    None   Some   Reasonable   Good   High   Very high

29. Pumpin, C, *The Essence of Corporate Strategy* (1987).

   None   Some   Reasonable   Good   High   Very high

Managing the Business Policy Process

30. *Development*
    General ability to manage the business policy development process.

    None   Some   Reasonable   Good   High   Very high

31. *Implementation*
    General ability to manage the achievement of business policy objectives.

    None   Some   Reasonable   Good   High   Very high

32. *Plans*
    General ability to create detailed formal business policy plans covering all the key functional areas.

    None   Some   Reasonable   Good   High   Very high

Ratios

There is a wide range of accounting or business ratios used to provide a measurement of performance by comparison over time either within a company or with other companies. What is your familiarity with the creation and interpretation of the following ratios?

For investors

	None	Some	Reasonable	Good	High	Very high
33. *Dividend yield*						
34. *Dividend cover*						
35. *Earnings yield*						
36. *Price to earnings ratio*						

For management – profitability

	None	Some	Reasonable	Good	High	Very high
37. *Return on capital employed*						
38. *Sales to capital employed*						
39. *Profit to sales*						
40. *Sales to fixed assets*						
41. *Sales to net current assets*						
42. *Sales to stocks*						
43. *Sales to debtors*						
44. *Creditors to sales*						

45. Debtors to average sales per day						
46. Cost of sales to average stocks						

For management – liquidity

	None	Some	Reasonable	Good	High	Very high
47. The current ratio – current assets to current liabilities						
48. The liquidity ratio – current assets less stocks to current liabilities						

Techniques and Systems

There are a number of overall business policy planning techniques which are sometimes described as 'systems'. What is your familiarity with the following?

	None	Some	Reasonable	Good	High	Very high
49. Ansoff system						
50. Argenti system						
51. Boston Consulting Group system						
52. Pumpin system						

Tools

There is a wide range of tools which can sometimes be of use in the development and implementation of business policy planning. What is your familiarity with the following selection?

	None	Some	Reasonable	Good	High	Very high
53. Competitive analysis						
54. Creativity techniques						
55. Cost benefit analysis						
56. Computer models – large scale						
57. Computer models for analysis						
58. Charts, profiles, matrices						
59. Critical path scheduling						
60. Decision analysis						
61. Discounted cash flow						
62. Evaluation tools						
63. Forecasting techniques						

	None	Some	Reasonable	Good	High	Very high
64. *Manpower planning*						
65. *Models and simulation – non-computer*						
66. *Management information systems*						
67. *Outcome matrix*						
68. *Programme budgets*						
69. *Risk analysis*						
70. *Sensitivity tests*						
71. *Utility theory*						

FUNCTIONAL SKILLS PROFILE C3
ORGANISING AND DEALING WITH PEOPLE ▶

Preamble

Listed below is a range of the skills involved in organising and dealing with people. Managers' skill levels vary considerably across the range and over time, but the skills are of general application for all managers.

We define organising and dealing with people as the ability to achieve results through people, preserving a balance between short, medium, and long-term goals of the business, and the need to retain staff morale and commitment.

Please read the list and consider it. Then ring the level of skill you feel that you have at present in each area. The broad comparison is with the skills needed as, say,

- a Chief Executive of a medium-sized business of, say, £20m to £30m turnover or 1,000 employees;

- a unit general manager in the NHS, for example, a Hospital General Manager;

- a Chief Executive of a District Council of, say, 100,000 population.

One would expect a capable and experienced senior manager to have a varying level of these skills depending on managerial level, specialisation, past training, and experience.

There is inevitably some overlap in many of the areas and room for some difference of view about definitions. The objective is to arrive at a reasonable overall self-assessment for your own use.

The ratings are as follows:

None   No significant level of skill and/or knowledge.

Some   Some knowledge and/or skill but lower than you would prefer.

Reasonable   Reasonable level of knowledge and/or skill enabling you to cope in that area without major difficulties.

Good   Good level of knowledge and/or skill enabling you to cope more than adequately. Probably about average for a senior manager in a medium-sized business.

High   High skill and/or knowledge level such as to encourage you to feel rather pleased with your performance.

Very high   Very high skill and/or knowledge level. You regard yourself as outstanding and your colleagues sometimes comment favourably.

We have subdivided the profile quite simply as follows:

- People one at a time — the units of management.
- People two at a time — issues of influence and authority.
- People in threes to twenties — efficiency and influence in groups.
- People in hundreds and thousands — issues of organisation and organisational design.

Obviously the division is not rigid, but it is useful.

People One at a Time

> 1. *Personality*
> Understanding of the main characteristics of human personality and how to appraise or measure those characteristics.
>
> None   Some   Reasonable   Good   High   Very high

2. *Behaviour*
   Understanding of the main organisational behaviour theories and the ability to use them in managing people.

   None   Some   Reasonable   Good   High   Very high

3. *Learning*
   Understanding of how people learn and of the concept of learning curves.

   None   Some   Reasonable   Good   High   Very high

4. *Appraisal*
   Ability to appraise personality and performance in a way which enhances performance.

   None   Some   Reasonable   Good   High   Very high

5. *Behaviour modification*
   Understanding of the way in which behaviour can be encouraged to change.

   None   Some   Reasonable   Good   High   Very high

6. *Adjusting to change*
   Understanding of the problems of change and of how individuals can be helped to adjust to it.

   None   Some   Reasonable   Good   High   Very high

7. *Development*
   Ability to judge individual development needs and help that development.

   None   Some   Reasonable   Good   High   Very high

8. *Discipline*
   Understanding of individual attitudes to discipline and of how to maintain discipline to enhance performance.

   None   Some   Reasonable   Good   High   Very high

9. *Control*
   Understanding of the issues involved in controlling individuals in ways which enhance performance.

   None   Some   Reasonable   Good   High   Very high

People Two at a Time

10. *Influence*
    Appreciation of the factors which affect influence in one-to-one relationships and how to handle them.

    None   Some   Reasonable   Good   High   Very high

11. *Behaviour change*
    Appreciation of how individuals in a one-to-one relationship seek to encourage behaviour change, and of how to handle those patterns.

    None   Some   Reasonable   Good   High   Very high

12. *Objectives*
    Appreciation of objective setting in one-to-one relationships and the ability to use that to improve performance.

    None   Some   Reasonable   Good   High   Very high

13. *Motivation*
    Appreciation of the motivation factors in one-to-one relationships and of how to deal with them.

    None   Some   Reasonable   Good   High   Very high

14. *Conflict*
    Appreciation of the dynamics of conflict in one-to-one relationships and of how to deal with those conflicts.

    None   Some   Reasonable   Good   High   Very high

ORGANISING AND DEALING WITH PEOPLE ▶ 123

People in Threes to Twenties

---

15. *Organisation development*
    Understanding of what organisation development is, of what the main techniques are, and of when to use them.

    None   Some   Reasonable   Good   High   Very high

---

16. *Participation and consultation*
    Understanding of human views on participation and consultation and the ability to meet those views in ways which enhance performance.

    None   Some   Reasonable   Good   High   Very high

---

17. *Team building*
    Understanding of the dynamics of teams and of team building.

    None   Some   Reasonable   Good   High   Very high

---

18. *Leadership style*
    Understanding of the variations in leadership style and the ability to use an appropriate style in varying circumstances.

    None   Some   Reasonable   Good   High   Very high

---

19. *Consensus*
    Understanding of the dynamics of consensus, its importance, and of how to encourage it in ways which improve performance.

    None   Some   Reasonable   Good   High   Very high

20. *Delegation*
    Appreciation of the principles of delegation and the ability to delegate while maintaining management control.

    None   Some   Reasonable   Good   High   Very high

21. *Organisational culture*
    Understanding of organisational culture, how to assess it, and how to engender culture change where necessary.

    None   Some   Reasonable   Good   High   Very high

22. *Groups*
    Awareness of the organisation of committees, teams, project teams, and working groups of all kinds, and the ability to create and use such groups effectively.

    None   Some   Reasonable   Good   High   Very high

ORGANISING AND DEALING WITH PEOPLE ▶ 125

23. *Decisions*
    Understanding of the decision-making process, the ability to make decisions, and help others to do so.

    None   Some   Reasonable   Good   High   Very high

People in Hundreds and Thousands

24. *Organisational structure and design*
    Awareness of the different types of organisation structure, the ability to design suitable structures and adjust them to meet changing business needs.

    None   Some   Reasonable   Good   High   Very high

25. *Communications*
    Awareness of the importance of communications inside the organisation and a knowledge of the methods of communication relevant to various organisation structures.

    None   Some   Reasonable   Good   High   Very high

26. *Manpower planning*
    Knowledge of manpower planning techniques and the ability to use them to ensure that the needs of the business are met.

    None   Some   Reasonable   Good   High   Very high

27. *Collective bargaining*
    Understanding of collective bargaining and of its management.

    None   Some   Reasonable   Good   High   Very high

28. *Decentralisation*
    Understanding of a decentralised organisation pattern and how to manage it.

    None   Some   Reasonable   Good   High   Very high

FUNCTIONAL SKILLS PROFILE C4
ACCOUNTING AND FINANCE ▶

Preamble

Listed below is a range of the skills involved in accounting and finance. The questionnaire is obviously designed for managers who have specialist skills in accounting and finance. Even with such managers the skill levels vary considerably across the range and over time.

Please read the list and consider it. Then ring the level of skill you feel that you have at present in each area. The broad comparison is with the skills needed as 'head of Accounting and Finance' in, say,

- a medium-sized business of, say, £20m to £30m turnover or around 1,000 employees;
- an NHS unit, for example, a hospital;
- a District Council of, say, 100,000 population.

One would expect a capable and experienced senior manager to have a varying level of these skills depending on managerial level, past training, and experience.

There is inevitably some overlap in many of the areas and room for some difference of view about definitions. The objective is to arrive at a reasonable overall self-assessment for your own use.

The ratings are as follows:

None No significant level of skill and/or knowledge.

Some Some knowledge and/or skill but lower than you would prefer.

Reasonable Level of knowledge and/or skill enabling you to cope in that area without major difficulties.

Good Good level of knowledge and/or skill enabling you to cope more than adequately. Probably about average for a senior manager in a medium-sized business.

High High skill and/or knowledge level such as to encourage you to feel rather pleased with your performance.

Very high Very high skill and/or knowledge level. You regard yourself as outstanding and your colleagues sometimes comment favourably.

The areas are subdivided and are not listed in order of importance.

Financial Accounts

1. *Statutory accounts – limited companies*
   Ability to prepare final accounts for limited companies.

   None   Some   Reasonable   Good   High   Very high

2. *Statutory accounts – groups*
   Ability to prepare group accounts.

   None   Some   Reasonable   Good   High   Very high

3. *Accounting standards*
   Up-to-date knowledge and understanding of accounting standards.

   None   Some   Reasonable   Good   High   Very high

4. *Company law*
   Working knowledge of the Companies Acts.

   None   Some   Reasonable   Good   High   Very high

5. *Current theory and practice*
   Knowledge and understanding of current development in accounting theory and standards.

   None   Some   Reasonable   Good   High   Very high

Tax

6. *Corporation tax – computations*
   Ability to prepare annual tax computations.

   None   Some   Reasonable   Good   High   Very high

7. *Corporation tax – planning*
   Ability to minimise future corporation tax liability through planning.

   None   Some   Reasonable   Good   High   Very high

8. *VAT*
   Up-to-date knowledge of the rules relating to VAT and opportunities for planning.

   None   Some   Reasonable   Good   High   Very high

9. *PAYE*
   Ability to operate PAYE.

   None   Some   Reasonable   Good   High   Very high

Management Accounts

10. *Preparation of management accounts*

    None   Some   Reasonable   Good   High   Very high

11. *Variance analysis*
    Working knowledge of the key volume and expenditure related variances.

    None   Some   Reasonable   Good   High   Very high

12. *Interpretation*
    Ability to interpret management accounts and provide guidance for management colleagues.

    None   Some   Reasonable   Good   High   Very high

Budgeting

13. *Cost/profit centre recognition*
    Ability to establish cost/profit centres and to recognise the need for responsibility and accountability.

    None   Some   Reasonable   Good   High   Very high

14. *Determination of costs*
    Ability to recognise the behaviour of costs (fixed/variable; direct/indirect).

    None   Some   Reasonable   Good   High   Very high

15. *Flexed budgets*
    Knowledge of the relationships between costs and volumes/units of activity.

    None   Some   Reasonable   Good   High   Very high

16. *Managing the budgeting process*
    Ability to control the preparation of budgets, recognising the need for participating and responsibility.

    None   Some   Reasonable   Good   High   Very high

Costing Systems

17. *Standard costing*
    Ability to operate standard costing systems.

    None   Some   Reasonable   Good   High   Very high

18. *Process costing*
    Ability to operate process costing systems.

    None   Some   Reasonable   Good   High   Very high

19. *Contract costing*
    Ability to operate contract costing systems.

    None   Some   Reasonable   Good   High   Very high

20. *Job costing*
    Ability to operate job costing systems.

    None   Some   Reasonable   Good   High   Very high

21. *Marginal and absorption costing*
    Degree of understanding of the differences between marginal and absorption costing.

    None   Some   Reasonable   Good   High   Very high

Treasury

22. *Cash flow forecasting*
    Ability to prepare, and subsequently monitor, detailed cash flow forecasts.

    None   Some   Reasonable   Good   High   Very high

23. *Foreign exchange*
    Ability to manage foreign exchange transactions.

    None   Some   Reasonable   Good   High   Very high

24. *Borrowing*
    Knowledge of the various types, uses and sources of loan finance.

    None   Some   Reasonable   Good   High   Very high

Investigation and Appraisal

25. *Acquisitions*
    Ability to evaluate and report upon potential acquisitions.

    None   Some   Reasonable   Good   High   Very high

26. *Project evaluation*
    Ability to evaluate and report upon new business projects.

    None   Some   Reasonable   Good   High   Very high

27. *Capital expenditure appraisal*
    Ability to evaluate and report upon new capital projects.

    None   Some   Reasonable   Good   High   Very high

28. *Techniques*
    Knowledge of the techniques used in evaluating new projects (discounted cash flow; internal rate of return; payback period).

    None   Some   Reasonable   Good   High   Very high

Secretarial

29. *Statutory duties*
    Working knowledge of the duties and responsibilities of the company secretary.

    None   Some   Reasonable   Good   High   Very high

Computers

30. *Hardware*
    Knowledge of the current developments in computer hardware.

    None   Some   Reasonable   Good   High   Very high

31. *Software*
    Knowledge of the current developments in computer software.

    None   Some   Reasonable   Good   High   Very high

32. *Applications packages*
    Knowledge of the range of available accounting applications packages.

    None   Some   Reasonable   Good   High   Very high

33. *Hands-on experience*
    Ability to use microcomputer-based decision-support systems (spreadsheets, databases, query languages).

    None   Some   Reasonable   Good   High   Very high

34. *Managing the DP environment*
    Ability to manage a business's data processing facilities.

    None   Some   Reasonable   Good   High   Very high

35. *Planning*
    Ability to plan a business's future data processing requirements.

    None   Some   Reasonable   Good   High   Very high

Systems

36. *Introduction of new systems*
    Ability to plan, design and implement new accounting systems.

    None   Some   Reasonable   Good   High   Very high

Planning

37. *Short-term planning*
    Ability to prepare short-term business plans, drawing upon the knowledge of functional departments such as sales and production.

    None   Some   Reasonable   Good   High   Very high

38. *Strategic planning*
    Ability to contribute to the long-term future of the business through the preparation of long-term business plans.

    None   Some   Reasonable   Good   High   Very high

39. *Techniques*
    Knowledge of the techniques of strategic planning.

    None   Some   Reasonable   Good   High   Very high

Pensions and insurance

40. *Pensions*
    Knowledge of the various types of pension scheme available and the ability to choose the most suitable.

    None   Some   Reasonable   Good   High   Very high

41. *Insurance*
    Ability to assess, in outline, the insurance requirements of a business given the need to comply with current legislation and to safeguard the business's assets and operation.

    None   Some   Reasonable   Good   High   Very high

Direction

42. *Goals*
Ability to set appropriate goals for the accounting and finance function within the company and obtain management's understanding and agreement to them.

None   Some   Reasonable   Good   High   Very high

43. *Plans*
Ability to create meaningful plans for the development of the accounting and finance function taking into account current facilities, current and future needs, and gain management's approval and support.

None   Some   Reasonable   Good   High   Very high

44. *Communication*
Ability to communicate with managers in order to appreciate their perspectives and increase their awareness of the accounting and finance function.

None   Some   Reasonable   Good   High   Very high

45. *Involvement*
Ability to obtain senior management's involvement in, and understanding of, their role in the application of accounting and finance information within the business.

None   Some   Reasonable   Good   High   Very high

Resources

46. *Skills assessment*
    Ability to assess the skills needed within the accounting and finance function, identify shortfalls, and justify recruitment.

    None   Some   Reasonable   Good   High   Very high

47. *Recruit*
    Ability to recruit the appropriate skills, at the appropriate compensation package.

    None   Some   Reasonable   Good   High   Very high

48. *Retain and train*
    Ability to retain and train accounting and finance staff by designing proper training programmes and providing career development.

    None   Some   Reasonable   Good   High   Very high

49. *Strategy*
    Ability to establish short and medium-term plans for the accounting and finance function within a long-term company strategy.

    None   Some   Reasonable   Good   High   Very high

50. *Selection*
   Ability to evaluate and select accounting and finance systems.

   None   Some   Reasonable   Good   High   Very high

51. *Budgeting*
   Ability to budget for the resources of the accounting and finance function, monitor expenditure and account for deviations.

   None   Some   Reasonable   Good   High   Very high

52. *Justification*
   Ability to establish a justification process for expenditure on the accounting and finance function.

   None   Some   Reasonable   Good   High   Very high

Effectiveness and Efficiency

53. *Accounting and finance environment*
   Ability to establish an accounting and finance environment which enhances effectiveness, efficiency and profits.

   None   Some   Reasonable   Good   High   Very high

54. *Cost-effectiveness*
    Ability to establish a cost-effective accounting and finance system and maintain that cost-effectiveness.

    None   Some   Reasonable   Good   High   Very high

Control and Accomplishment

55. *Planning*
    Ability to establish an overall accounting and finance function plan in collaboration with senior management, and control its implementation with good levels of communication both within and outside the accounting and finance function.

    None   Some   Reasonable   Good   High   Very high

56. *Quality control*
    Ability to maintain at high quality the work produced by the accounting and finance function as evidenced by management satisfaction.

    None   Some   Reasonable   Good   High   Very high

FUNCTIONAL SKILLS PROFILE C5
OPERATIONS ▶

Preamble

Listed below is a range of the skills involved in operations. The questionnaire is obviously designed for managers who have specialist skills in operations. Even with such managers the skill levels vary considerably across the range and over time.

Please read the list and consider it. Then tick or ring the level of skill you feel that you have at present in each area. The broad comparison is with the skills needed as 'head of Operations' in, say,

- a medium-sized business of, say, £20m to £30m turnover or around 1,000 employees;
- an NHS unit, for example, a hospital;
- a District Council of, say, 100,000 population.

One would expect a capable and experienced senior manager to have a varying level of these skills depending on managerial level, past training, and experience.

There is inevitably some overlap in many of the areas and room for some difference of view about definitions. The objective is to arrive at a reasonable overall self-assessment for your own use.

The ratings are as follows:

None No significant level of skill and/or knowledge.

Some Some knowledge and/or skill but lower than you would prefer.

Reasonable Reasonable level of knowledge and/or skill enabling you to cope in that area without major difficulties.

Good Good level of knowledge and/or skill enabling you to cope more than adequately. Probably about average for a senior manager in a medium-sized business.

High High skill and/or knowledge level such as to encourage you to feel rather pleased with your performance.

Very high Very high skill and/or knowledge level. You regard yourself as outstanding and your colleagues sometimes comment favourably.

The areas are subdivided and are not listed in order of importance.

Production Types

An understanding of the main types of production and of the differences between them.

	None	Some	Reasonable	Good	High	Very high
1. One-off production						
2. Batch production						
3. Flow production						
4. Process production						
5. Modular production						

Production Control

A knowledge of the key areas of production control which is concerned with managing the production of goods in the right sequence in the least time and at the lowest cost.

	None	Some	Reasonable	Good	High	Very high
6. Stock control/ inventory control						
7. Production control						

	None	Some	Reasonable	Good	High	Very high
8. Warehouse operation and management						
9. Sourcing						
10. Machine loading						
11. Line balancing						
12. Make or buy decision criteria						
13. Materials management						
14. Monitoring and progressing						

Production Study

A knowledge of the key areas of production study which we define as the analytical study of production with a view to improving productivity.

	None	Some	Reasonable	Good	High	Very high
15. Method study						
16. Time study						
17. Incentive payment design						

Industrial Engineering

A knowledge of the key areas of industrial engineering which is a generic term for techniques aimed at the physical and organisational aspects of the production set-up, and intended to engender high levels of productivity at low levels of cost.

	None	Some	Reasonable	Good	High	Very high
18. Plant layout						
19. Automation						
20. Plant selection						
21. Production line design						
22. Group technology						
23. Product design with respect to ease of production						
24. Value analysis						
25. Robotics						
26. Jig and tool – use and design						
27. Materials handling						

Cost

	None	Some	Reasonable	Good	High	Very high
28. Costing						
29. Capital investment appraisal						
30. Cost controls						

Quality Control

An understanding of the key areas of quality control which we define here as the techniques designed to ensure that products are of acceptable quality at minimum production cost, and minimising quality control cost.

	None	Some	Reasonable	Good	High	Very high
31. Quality control charts						
32. Inspection methods						
33. Statistical quality control techniques						
34. Quality standards						

People

	None	Some	Reasonable	Good	High	Very high
35. *Incentive maintenance*						
36. *Employee relations*						
37. *Health and safety at work*						
38. *Motivation*						
39. *Job design*						

Organisation

40. *Organisation structures*
    Knowledge of available organisation structures and of their suitability for particular situations.

    None   Some   Reasonable   Good   High   Very high

41. *Production management*

    None   Some   Reasonable   Good   High   Very high

42. *Production supervision*

    None   Some   Reasonable   Good   High   Very high

Maintenance

43. Understanding of the main aspects of maintenance techniques and of the relationship between maintenance methods, maintenance costs, production continuity, and production costs.

None   Some   Reasonable   Good   High   Very high

Computer-based Techniques

A knowledge of the main computer-based techniques relevant to production. The terms and techniques frequently overlap and, of course, overlap the other areas in this profile.

	None	Some	Reasonable	Good	High	Very high
44. Computer aided production management						
45. Computer aided manufacture						
46. Computer integrated manufacture						
47. Advanced manufacturing technology						
48. Just In Time						
49. Flexible manufacturing systems						

	None	Some	Reasonable	Good	High	Very high
50. Computer aided process planning						
51. CNC tools						
52. Expert systems						
53. Real time machine loading						

FUNCTIONAL SKILLS PROFILE C6
MARKETING AND SALES ▶

Preamble
Listed below is a range of the skills involved in marketing and sales. The questionnaire is obviously designed for managers who have specialist skills in marketing or sales or both. Even with such managers the skill levels vary considerably across the range and over time.

Please read the list and consider it. Then ring the level of skill you feel that you have at present in each area. The broad comparison is with the skills needed as 'head of Marketing and Sales' in, say,

- a medium-sized business of, say, £20m to £30m turnover or around 1,000 employees;
- an NHS unit, for example, a hospital;
- a District Council of, say, 100,000 population.

One would expect a capable and experienced senior manager to have a varying level of these skills depending on managerial level, past training, and experience.

There is inevitably some overlap in many of the areas and room for some difference of view about definitions. The objective is to arrive at a reasonable overall self-assessment for your own use.

The ratings are as follows:

None   No significant level of skill and/or knowledge.

Some   Some knowledge and/or skill but lower than you would prefer.

Reasonable   Reasonable level of knowledge and/or skill enabling you to cope in that area without major difficulties.

Good   Good level of knowledge and/or skill enabling you to cope more than adequately. Probably about average for a senior manager in a medium-sized business.

High   High skill and/or knowledge level such as to encourage you to feel rather pleased with your performance.

Very high   Very high skill and/or knowledge level. You regard yourself as outstanding and your colleagues sometimes comment favourably.

The areas are subdivided and are not listed in order of importance.

Marketing and Sales

The necessary marketing and sales skills for considering and documenting business policy plans. There are a wide range of these and the ones below are particularly important. Wherever the words 'your market' or 'your products' are used they mean those relevant to your present company.

Knowledge – Marketing

1. *Market size*
   Up-to-date knowledge of the size of your market and any sector within it.

   None   Some   Reasonable   Good   High   Very high

2. *Market share*
   Up-to-date knowledge of brand shares in your market, their history and forecast potential.

   None   Some   Reasonable   Good   High   Very high

3. *Product – benefits*
   Up-to-date knowledge of the benefits of your products and their comparative strengths and weaknesses.

   None   Some   Reasonable   Good   High   Very high

4. *Consumer profile and penetration*
   Up-to-date knowledge of consumer profile and penetration of all your brands.

   None   Some   Reasonable   Good   High   Very high

5. *Buyer and user attitudes*
   Up-to-date awareness of buyer and user attitudes towards companies and their products generally.

   None   Some   Reasonable   Good   High   Very high

6. *Packaging*
   Up-to-date knowledge of packaging forms, their costs and potential developments.

   None   Some   Reasonable   Good   High   Very high

7. *Product development*
   Up-to-date knowledge of trends in new product development generally.

   None   Some   Reasonable   Good   High   Very high

8. *Risk appraisal*
   Up-to-date knowledge of the methods of risk appraisal.

   None   Some   Reasonable   Good   High   Very high

9. *Manufacturing*
   Up-to-date knowledge of manufacturing methods in relevant products and materials and potential improvements.

   None   Some   Reasonable   Good   High   Very high

10. *Distribution*
    Up-to-date knowledge of channels of distribution generally and their costs.

    None   Some   Reasonable   Good   High   Very high

11. *Trading policy*
    Up-to-date knowledge of prices, discounts, special terms and margins for all levels of the manufacturing and distribution chain for your products.

    None   Some   Reasonable   Good   High   Very high

12. *Legal*
    Up-to-date knowledge of legislative and other controls.

    None   Some   Reasonable   Good   High   Very high

13. *Research*
    Up-to-date knowledge of the sources and validity of published data and of specialist research organisations in your market.

    None   Some   Reasonable   Good   High   Very high

Techniques

14. *Forecasting*
    Up-to-date knowledge of monitoring and forecasting statistical techniques.

    None   Some   Reasonable   Good   High   Very high

15. *Costing*
    Up-to-date knowledge of product costing methods and how, when and where to apply them.

    None   Some   Reasonable   Good   High   Very high

Knowledge – Communications

16. *Communications*
    Up-to-date knowledge of advertising, public relations, promotions, direct response, literature, exhibitions, sponsorship and after sales support techniques.

    None   Some   Reasonable   Good   High   Very high

17. *Advertising*
    Up-to-date knowledge of selecting and costing advertising in the broadcast and printed media and of measuring their effectiveness.

    None   Some   Reasonable   Good   High   Very high

18. *Public relations*
    Up-to-date knowledge of selecting and costing public relations activities and of measuring their effectiveness.

    None   Some   Reasonable   Good   High   Very high

19. *Promotions and other communications activities*
    Up-to-date knowledge of selecting and costing other communications activities and promotions and of measuring their effectiveness.

    None   Some   Reasonable   Good   High   Very high

20. *Literature*
    Up-to-date knowledge of the production methods and costs of appropriate sales literature.

    None   Some   Reasonable   Good   High   Very high

21. *Conferences and meetings*
    Up-to-date knowledge of the organisation, direction and costing of conferences and meetings.

    None   Some   Reasonable   Good   High   Very high

22. *Competitors communications spends*
    Up-to-date knowledge of the communications activities, spends and performance of competitors.

    None   Some   Reasonable   Good   High   Very high

Knowledge – Selling

23. *Selling techniques*
    Up-to-date knowledge of professional sales techniques.

    None   Some   Reasonable   Good   High   Very high

24. *Sales statistics*
    Up-to-date knowledge of the methods of monitoring sales data and their analysis.

    None   Some   Reasonable   Good   High   Very high

25. *Salesforce – targeting*
    Up-to-date knowledge of the methods of salesforce targeting and measurement by product, geography and buyer.

    None   Some   Reasonable   Good   High   Very high

26. *Salesforce – planning*
    Up-to-date knowledge of journey planning techniques and control.

    None   Some   Reasonable   Good   High   Very high

27. *Salesforce – remuneration*
    Up-to-date knowledge of the alternative methods and costs of remunerating salesmen.

    None   Some   Reasonable   Good   High   Very high

28. *Key accounts*
    Up-to-date knowledge of key account companies in your market, their buyers and their needs.

    None   Some   Reasonable   Good   High   Very high

Planning

29. *Short-term planning*
    Ability to prepare short-term business plans, drawing upon the knowledge of functional departments such as accounts and production.

    None   Some   Reasonable   Good   High   Very high

30. *Strategic planning*
    Ability to contribute to the long-term future of a business through the preparation of long-term business plans.

    None   Some   Reasonable   Good   High   Very high

31. *Techniques*
    Knowledge of the techniques of strategic planning.

    None   Some   Reasonable   Good   High   Very high

Direction

32. *Goals*
    Ability to set appropriate goals for the marketing/sales function within a company and obtain management's understanding and agreement to them.

    None   Some   Reasonable   Good   High   Very high

33. *Plans*
    Ability to create meaningful plans for the development of the marketing/sales function in a company, taking into account current facilities, current and future needs, and gain management's approval and support.

    None   Some   Reasonable   Good   High   Very high

34. *Communication*
    Ability to communicate with managers in order to appreciate their perspectives and increase their awareness of the marketing/sales function.

    None   Some   Reasonable   Good   High   Very high

35. *Involvement*
   Ability to obtain senior management's involvement in, and understanding of, their role in the application of marketing/sales information within the business.

   None   Some   Reasonable   Good   High   Very high

36. *Skills assessment*
   Ability to assess the skills needed within the marketing/sales function, evaluate strengths and weaknesses and justify training and recruitment.

   None   Some   Reasonable   Good   High   Very high

Resources

37. *Recruit*
   Ability to recruit the appropriate skills, at the appropriate remuneration package.

   None   Some   Reasonable   Good   High   Very high

38. *Retain and train – internal*
   Ability to retain and train marketing/sales staff by designing proper training programmes and providing career development.

   None   Some   Reasonable   Good   High   Very high

39. *Retain and train – external*
    Ability to retain and train distributors, wholesalers, and retailers by designing proper training programmes about the company and its products.

    None   Some   Reasonable   Good   High   Very high

40. *Strategy*
    Ability to establish short and medium-term plans for the marketing/sales function within a long-term company strategy.

    None   Some   Reasonable   Good   High   Very high

41. *Selection*
    Ability to evaluate and select appropriate marketing/sales structures.

    None   Some   Reasonable   Good   High   Very high

42. *Budgeting*
    Ability to budget for marketing/sales function resources, monitor expenditure and account for deviations.

    None   Some   Reasonable   Good   High   Very high

43. *Justification*
    Ability to establish a justification process for expenditure on the marketing/sales function.

    None   Some   Reasonable   Good   High   Very high

Effectiveness and Efficiency

44. *Marketing and sales*
    Ability to provide a marketing and sales environment which gives high management satisfaction.

    None   Some   Reasonable   Good   High   Very high

45. *Analysis*
    Ability to establish analysis routines which can identify variations in performance promptly and provide information for the creation of new ones.

    None   Some   Reasonable   Good   High   Very high

46. *Achievement of targets*
    Ability to achieve planned targets within the cost and time-scales set.

    None   Some   Reasonable   Good   High   Very high

47. *Products improvement*
    Ability to improve and update products and services as measured by increased market shares or other above market average performance measures.

    None   Some   Reasonable   Good   High   Very high

48. *Corporate image and awareness*
    Ability to improve the market's attitudes towards a company's image and products.

    None   Some   Reasonable   Good   High   Very high

49. *Policy*
    Ability to review sales/marketing systems, products and communications to ensure that they accord with company policy, are up to date, easy to use and remain legally valid.

    None   Some   Reasonable   Good   High   Very high

50. *Cost-effectiveness*
    Ability to establish a cost-effective marketing and sales function and maintain that cost-effectiveness.

    None   Some   Reasonable   Good   High   Very high

Control and Accomplishment

51. *Planning*
    Ability to establish an overall marketing and sales function plan in collaboration with senior management, and to control its implementation with good levels of communication both within and outside the marketing and sales function.

    None   Some   Reasonable   Good   High   Very high

52. *Quality control*
    Ability to maintain at high quality the work produced by the marketing and sales function as evidenced by management satisfaction.

    None   Some   Reasonable   Good   High   Very high

53. *Development*
    Ability to monitor activities in the market place to ensure that products and the sales/marketing function are developed in a manner which will secure the long-term objectives.

    None   Some   Reasonable   Good   High   Very high

FUNCTIONAL SKILLS PROFILE C7
RESEARCH AND PRODUCT DEVELOPMENT ▶

Preamble

Listed below is a range of the skills and experience required to manage basic research in areas likely to be relevant to your business area/or the ability to manage the initiation and development of new products from conceptual stage to manufacture in your company's area of business.

Please read the list and consider it. Then ring the level of skill and/or knowledge you feel that you have at present in each area.

The broad comparison is with the skill needed as 'head of Research' or 'Product Development' or 'Research and Development' in a medium-sized business of, say, £20m to £30m turnover or around 1,000 employees. Even with such managers the skill levels naturally vary considerably across the range and over time. One would expect a capable and experienced senior manager to have a varying level of these skills depending on managerial level, past training and experience.

There is inevitably some overlap in many areas and room for some difference of view about definitions. The objective is to arrive at a reasonable overall self-assessment for your own use.

The ratings are as follows:

None No significant level of skill and/or knowledge.

Some Some knowledge and/or skill but lower than you would prefer.

Reasonable Reasonable level of knowledge and/or skill enabling you to cope in that area without major difficulties.

Good Good level of knowledge and/or skill enabling you to cope more than adequately. Probably about average for a senior manager in a medium-sized business.

High High skill and/or knowledge level such as to encourage you to feel rather pleased with your performance.

Very high   Very high skill and/or knowledge level. You regard yourself as outstanding and your colleagues sometimes comment favourably.

The areas are subdivided and are not listed in order of importance.

Contemporary Knowledge (State-of-the-art)

1. *Applied research*
   Knowledge or experience of the development of applied research in universities, research centres, science parks and innovation centres, and the process of technology transfer.

   None   Some   Reasonable   Good   High   Very high

2. *New technology*
   Level of skill in keeping yourself abreast of developments in new technology and relating these to product development.

   None   Some   Reasonable   Good   High   Very high

3. *Staff awareness*
   Level of experience in ensuring your staff are trained and developed to maximise the use of research findings and available new technology.

   None   Some   Reasonable   Good   High   Very high

4. *New materials and processes*
   Knowledge of the development of new materials and production processes which can significantly affect research and product development activities including design.

   None   Some   Reasonable   Good   High   Very high

5. *Properties of materials*
   Familiarity with the properties of the materials used in the company's products, eg steels, plastics, paints, lubricants.

   None   Some   Reasonable   Good   High   Very high

6. *Potential of inventions*
   Inventions – skill in determining their commercial potential, and identifying relevant by-products or offshoots.

   None   Some   Reasonable   Good   High   Very high

Competitors

7. *Research and development plans*
   Skill or experience in determining competitors' research and development plans, capability and direction, by reference to their product literature, exhibition material, or published research data.

   None   Some   Reasonable   Good   High   Very high

8. *Legal and ethical constraints*
   Knowledge of the legal restraints in obtaining competitor intelligence, and the ethical standards which prevail in your industry's area of business.

   None   Some   Reasonable   Good   High   Very high

9. *Intellectual property*
   Knowledge of the legal requirements and practical difficulties in ensuring intellectual property protection for your own business.

   None   Some   Reasonable   Good   High   Very high

Strategy

10. *Direction of change*
    Skill in predicting the direction of technological change and forecasting probable capabilities and opportunities for your company.

    None   Some   Reasonable   Good   High   Very high

11. *Formulation of strategy*
    Skill or experience in formulating a research and product development strategy by reference to corporate objectives, current knowledge, capability and marketing information.

    None   Some   Reasonable   Good   High   Very high

12. *Need and purpose*
    Understanding the need for an agreed strategy which identifies its major purpose, which may include cost reduction, better product performance, product divergence, market growth.

    None   Some   Reasonable   Good   High   Very high

13. *Corporate planning techniques*
    Understanding of corporate planning techniques used in research and product development, eg gap analysis, risk analysis, capability analysis.

    None   Some   Reasonable   Good   High   Very high

Knowledge or experience of strategy types, utilised by Research and Development:

14. *Offensive strategies*
    Offensive strategies, where the launch of a new product could ensure a rapid growth in market share or would seriously damage a market leader.

    None   Some   Reasonable   Good   High   Very high

15. *Defensive strategies*
    Defensive strategies, where research and product development serve to reduce manufacturing costs and ultimately retain market share.

    None   Some   Reasonable   Good   High   Very high

16. *Radical innovation*
    Long-term technological change, where a major research and product development programme is geared towards radical innovation in product application purposes, and seeks to alter or remove entirely conventional product thinking.

    None   Some   Reasonable   Good   High   Very high

17. *Competitor weakness*
    Competitor weakness, where product development is designed to attack omissions or deficiencies in product lines available from competitors or the market leader.

    None   Some   Reasonable   Good   High   Very high

Licensing, which takes two forms:

18. Licensing developed R & D from another company in order to reduce one's own R & D expenditure, or to divert one's own expenditure to a more rewarding activity.

    None   Some   Reasonable   Good   High   Very high

19. Licensing one's own development to other companies in order to divert competitors from an offensive strategy they may be assuming.

    None   Some   Reasonable   Good   High   Very high

20. *Market reduction*
    Growth through market reduction, which involves launching a new technological product at the right time, and although this will result in an overall market reduction, will serve to increase your company's sector of that market.

    None   Some   Reasonable   Good   High   Very high

Creativity

21. *Encouraging creativity*
    Ability to ensure the creative capability of staff is identified and encouraged, and that an environment exists in which innovation is not suppressed by previous practice, but at the same time does not consume an unacceptable amount of time or budget allocation.

    None   Some   Reasonable   Good   High   Very high

22. *External input*
    Ensure ideas and suggestions from outside the research and product development departments are adequately considered and incorporated.

    None   Some   Reasonable   Good   High   Very high

23. *Analytical techniques*
    Knowledge of developed analytical problem-solving techniques including attribute analysis, morphological analysis and modelling.

    None   Some   Reasonable   Good   High   Very high

24. *Non-analytical techniques*
    Knowledge of non-analytical techniques, including lateral thinking, syntactics and brainstorming.

    None   Some   Reasonable   Good   High   Very high

Planning

25. *Constructing a programme*
    Skill or experience in building a research and product development programme which will ensure products are available at the right quality, time and cost, and devising appropriate action plans.

    None   Some   Reasonable   Good   High   Very high

26. *Analysis of marketing data*
    Skill or experience in analysing current sales/marketing data in order to amend research and product development plans as necessary.

    None   Some   Reasonable   Good   High   Very high

27. *Product obsolescence*
    Understanding of product life-cycles and obsolescence trends to plan research and product development activity.

    None   Some   Reasonable   Good   High   Very high

28. *Analysis of sales data*
    Ability to analyse historical sales information in order to predict market capture by new products, and relating these to research and product development time-scales.

    None   Some   Reasonable   Good   High   Very high

29. *The needs of others*
    Ability to work closely with suppliers, customers and end-users to understand the impact their needs and problems may have on your research and product development plans.

    None   Some   Reasonable   Good   High   Very high

30. *Commercial requirements*
    Ability to formulate project selection and evaluation systems by reference to return on investment and long-term commercial potential.

    None   Some   Reasonable   Good   High   Very high

Resources and Control

31. *Justifying investment*
    Skill or experience in formulating justifications for revenue or capital expenditure on research and product development projects.

    None   Some   Reasonable   Good   High   Very high

32. *Monitoring expenditure*
    Ability to ensure budget resource allocation is monitored closely and frequently against original plans and against changing market requirements.

    None   Some   Reasonable   Good   High   Very high

33. *Manpower levels*
    Skill or experience in recruiting and retaining staff with relevant experience and qualifications to ensure the manpower resource is related to agreed research and product development plans.

    None   Some   Reasonable   Good   High   Very high

34. *Manpower quality*
    Skill or experience in determining training and development needs for existing staff in order to meet the changing needs of the development plan.

    None   Some   Reasonable   Good   High   Very high

35. *Motivating*
    Skill or experience in rewarding and motivating staff in order to maximise their contribution.

    None   Some   Reasonable   Good   High   Very high

36. *Project control techniques*
    Knowledge of the range of developed techniques for project control including critical path analysis.

    None   Some   Reasonable   Good   High   Very high

Design and Testing

37. *Feasibility studies*
    Skill or experience in devising feasibility studies.

    None   Some   Reasonable   Good   High   Very high

38. *Design technology*
    Knowledge of the range of contemporary design techniques available including CAD, graphics, systems modelling.

    None   Some   Reasonable   Good   High   Very high

39. *Hazard testing*
    Knowledge of hazard analysis techniques to evaluate the performance of the product in improbable but statistically possible situations.

    None   Some   Reasonable   Good   High   Very high

40. *Just In Time*
    Familiarity with the concepts of Just In Time manufacture and how that affects the design approach.

    None   Some   Reasonable   Good   High   Very high

41. *Data capture and analysis*
    Skill or experience in using computerised data collection and analysis.

    None   Some   Reasonable   Good   High   Very high

42. *Statistical analysis*
    Ability to use statistical techniques for analysis purposes.

    None   Some   Reasonable   Good   High   Very high

43. *Simulation*
    Skill or experience in using simulation techniques for product testing.

    None   Some   Reasonable   Good   High   Very high

RESEARCH AND PRODUCT DEVELOPMENT ▶ 177

44. *Field trials*
    Skill or experience in initiating a field trials programme and analysing the relevant data produced.

    None   Some   Reasonable   Good   High   Very high

45. *After-sales evaluation*
    Skill or experience in ensuring post-launch evaluations are set up in order to overcome potential design, quality or application difficulties.

    None   Some   Reasonable   Good   High   Very high

Commitment and Communication

46. *Promoting the function*
    Skill in promoting research and product development's place in the business, and gaining commitment from heads of other functions.

    None   Some   Reasonable   Good   High   Very high

47. *Working together*
    Experience of chairing a task force or product launch committee which will ensure needs of marketing, manufacturing, packaging and distribution are taken into account throughout all development stages.

    None   Some   Reasonable   Good   High   Very high

FUNCTIONAL SKILLS PROFILE C8
PERSONNEL AND EMPLOYEE RELATIONS ▶

Preamble

Listed below is a range of the skills and experience involved in personnel and employee relations. The questionnaire is obviously designed for managers who have specialist skills in personnel and employee relations. Even with such managers the skill levels vary considerably across the range and over time.

Please read the list and consider it. Then ring the level of skill and/or knowledge you feel that you have at present in each area. The broad comparison is with the skills needed as 'head of Personnel and Employee Relations' in, say,

- a medium-sized business of, say, £20m to £30m turnover or around 1,000 employees;
- an NHS unit, for example, a hospital;
- a District Council of, say, 100,000 population.

One would expect a capable and experienced senior manager to have a varying level of these skills depending on managerial level, past training, and experience. There is inevitably some overlap in many areas and room for some difference of view about definitions. The objective is to arrive at a reasonable overall self-assessment for your own use.

The ratings are as follows:

None No significant level of skill and/or knowledge.

Some Some knowledge and/or skill but lower than you would prefer.

Reasonable Reasonable level of knowledge and/or skill enabling you to cope in that area without major difficulties.

Good Good level of knowledge and/or skill enabling you to cope more than adequately. Probably about average for a senior manager in a medium-sized business.

High   High skill and/or knowledge level such as to encourage you to feel rather pleased with your performance.

Very high   Very high skill and/or knowledge level. You regard yourself as outstanding and your colleagues sometimes comment favourably.

The areas are subdivided and are not listed in order of importance.

General

1. *Human resources policies*
   Ability to formulate and implement policies which contribute effectively to the best use of human resources and, therefore, the organisation's viability, while maintaining social and legal responsibilities, in the following areas:

   a) Manpower planning, appraisal, training and development, recruitment and selection.

   None   Some   Reasonable   Good   High   Very high

   b) Employee relations, employment law, communications.

   None   Some   Reasonable   Good   High   Very high

   c) Wage and salary administration.

   None   Some   Reasonable   Good   High   Very high

d) Health and safety, employee services, benefits, welfare.

    None   Some   Reasonable   Good   High   Very high

2. *Variety of needs*
   Ability to establish and maintain a personnel and employee relations function in an organisation where several activities exist, separated by geographical location and/or product type and/or industry.

   None   Some   Reasonable   Good   High   Very high

3. *Values and behaviour*
   Awareness of the social, ethnic, cultural and moral values which affect behaviour and relationships in the workplace.

   None   Some   Reasonable   Good   High   Very high

4. *Case studies*
   Knowledge of traditional and contemporary studies in conflict, motivation and morale, and their contribution to contemporary views in human resource management.

   None   Some   Reasonable   Good   High   Very high

Manpower Planning

5. *Analytical techniques*
   Knowledge of analysis techniques to identify productivity, capacity, costs and utilisation, and the need for improvement.

   None   Some   Reasonable   Good   High   Very high

6. *Future needs*
   Ability to estimate future manpower demand by reference to plans of the business, and predicted levels of activity.

   None   Some   Reasonable   Good   High   Very high

7. *Future supply*
   Ability to estimate future manpower supply based on present quality and quantity, and predicted changes.

   None   Some   Reasonable   Good   High   Very high

8. *Formulating manpower plans*
   Experience of formulating plans aimed at resolving deficits/surpluses in manpower, cost, utilisation or productivity.

   None   Some   Reasonable   Good   High   Very high

9. *Implementing plans*
   Experience of monitoring the implementation of manpower plans, and adjusting for variances.

   None   Some   Reasonable   Good   High   Very high

Appraisal, Training and Development

10. *Assessing performance*
    Ability to develop and maintain regular effective procedures for monitoring and evaluating employee performance.

    None   Some   Reasonable   Good   High   Very high

11. *Identifying deficiencies*
    Ability to identify personal, sectional or organisational deficiencies revealed by appraisal procedures, and which may be corrected by training or development.

    None   Some   Reasonable   Good   High   Very high

12. *Management succession*
    Ability to identify the development needs arising from a management succession or career plan.

    None   Some   Reasonable   Good   High   Very high

13. *Training needs*
    Ability to identify craft apprentice, administrative and technical training needs by reference to line management and to manpower plans.

    None   Some   Reasonable   Good   High   Very high

14. *Objectives*
    Ability to define the objectives of a training and development plan, and prepare an annual programme.

    None   Some   Reasonable   Good   High   Very high

15. *In-house training*
    Personal experience of running a training course or series of seminars, with particular reference to supervisory and managerial needs.

    None   Some   Reasonable   Good   High   Very high

16. *External training*
    Knowledge of the variety of training courses and centres, management development colleges, business schools, adventure-based activities, and the ability to make an effective choice.

    None   Some   Reasonable   Good   High   Very high

17. *Controlling costs*
    Ability to budget and control training costs, including satisfying the requirements of an Industry Training Board.

    None   Some   Reasonable   Good   High   Very high

18. *Evaluation and monitoring*
    Ability to establish and maintain an effective system for monitoring and evaluating a training/development programme, and identifying actual changes in organisation performance.

    None   Some   Reasonable   Good   High   Very high

Recruitment and Selection

19. *Internal transfer*
    By reference to manpower plans, ability to recommend transfer/promotion to fill initial vacancies.

    None   Some   Reasonable   Good   High   Very high

20. *Defining the job*
    Knowledge of job analysis and job design techniques, and preparing job/person specification.

    None   Some   Reasonable   Good   High   Very high

21. *Seeking externally*
    Ability to draft advertisement copy, select appropriate recruitment media and use external recruitment agencies and consultants.

    None   Some   Reasonable   Good   High   Very high

22. *Conducting interviews*
    Ability to determine the most appropriate interview mechanism for a particular vacancy, and ensure it is conducted satisfactorily to meet the needs of both applicant and functional management.

    None   Some   Reasonable   Good   High   Very high

23. *Selection exercises*
    Training in, and application of, other selection techniques, eg aptitude/ability tests, skills and personality profiles, group exercises.

    None   Some   Reasonable   Good   High   Very high

24. *Assessing candidates*
    Ability to write concise and objective candidate assessments, and present short-lists to functional management.

    None   Some   Reasonable   Good   High   Very high

25. *Recruitment campaigns*
    Experience of planning major recruitment campaigns conducted away from the company base, including university/college 'milk round'.

    None   Some   Reasonable   Good   High   Very high

Employee Relations

26. *Third parties*
    Knowledge of trade union organisation and the workings of employers' associations.

    None   Some   Reasonable   Good   High   Very high

27. *Relating to representatives*
    Ability to relate to and reach a rapid rapport with blue and white collar representatives, management and full-time officials of trade unions.

    None   Some   Reasonable   Good   High   Very high

28. *Negotiations*
    Experience of negotiating a management proposal which changes terms, conditions, or practices of employment of a major group of employees, including annual negotiations.

    None   Some   Reasonable   Good   High   Very high

29. *Procedures*
    Ability to develop, evolve and police, collective bargaining, grievance and disciplinary procedures.

    None   Some   Reasonable   Good   High   Very high

30. *Resolving stoppages*
    Personal experience in resolving a work stoppage, either unofficial or official.

    None   Some   Reasonable   Good   High   Very high

31. *Introducing radical change*
    Experience of negotiating the introduction of new technology or other significant automation/computerisation.

    None   Some   Reasonable   Good   High   Very high

32. *Effecting redundancies*
    Experience of successfully negotiating/implementing a redundancy programme.

    None   Some   Reasonable   Good   High   Very high

33. *Carrying out dismissals*
Experience of effecting dismissal(s) without adverse legal or trade union reaction.

None   Some   Reasonable   Good   High   Very high

34. *Predicting issues*
Ability to identify and predict major industrial relations problems by interpretation of apparently minor grievances or actions.

None   Some   Reasonable   Good   High   Very high

35. *Resolving conflict*
Ability to identify long-term or deep-rooted areas of conflict between management and trade union representatives and formulate a strategy for resolving.

None   Some   Reasonable   Good   High   Very high

Employment Law

36. *Equal opportunities*
Working knowledge of equal opportunity (sex and race) legislation, and equal pay/equal value legislation.

None   Some   Reasonable   Good   High   Very high

37. *Employment statutes*
    Working knowledge of Employment Acts and redundancy payments legislation.

    None   Some   Reasonable   Good   High   Very high

38. *Other relevant law*
    Working knowledge of common law and the laws of contract.

    None   Some   Reasonable   Good   High   Very high

39. *Legal decisions*
    Ability to maintain an up-to-date knowledge of court and tribunal findings, identify those relevant legal decisions and recommend the necessary course of action for line management.

    None   Some   Reasonable   Good   High   Very high

40. *Statutory institutions*
    Knowledge of the working of employment law institutions, ie ACAS, EAT, tribunals.

    None   Some   Reasonable   Good   High   Very high

41. *Tribunal presentation*
    Experience of successfully presenting a case at a tribunal.

    None   Some   Reasonable   Good   High   Very high

42. *Outside the UK*
    Working knowledge of employment laws and practices in other EC countries, and further afield, including those affecting expatriate personnel.

    None   Some   Reasonable   Good   High   Very high

Communications

43. *Briefing groups*
    Ability to construct and maintain a briefing group, or similar, structure.

    None   Some   Reasonable   Good   High   Very high

44. *Joint consultation*
    Experience of operating a joint consultation system independently of, or instead of, union/management procedures.

    None   Some   Reasonable   Good   High   Very high

45. *Innovation*
    Ability to introduce innovative techniques in daily employee information needs, eg use of video, broadcast, notices, and bulletins.

    None   Some   Reasonable   Good   High   Very high

46. *Staff information*
    Ability to produce a company newsletter, house journal, employee handbook, etc.

    None   Some   Reasonable   Good   High   Very high

47. *Company reports*
    Experience of producing an annual report for employees, identifying company performance and results in a simple, attractive and readable format.

    None   Some   Reasonable   Good   High   Very high

Wage and Salary Administration

48. *Remuneration policy*
    Appreciation of the fundamental objectives of a wages and salaries policy, and the variety of payments systems available with their respective dangers and advantages.

    None   Some   Reasonable   Good   High   Very high

49. *Reward surveys*
    Ability to conduct wage and salary surveys and to interpret professionally published comparisons.

    None   Some   Reasonable   Good   High   Very high

50. *Job evaluation techniques*
    Knowledge of the variety of job evaluation techniques, with their respective attributes and difficulties.

    None   Some   Reasonable   Good   High   Very high

51. *Job evaluation schemes*
    Experience of administering a job evaluation scheme, including monitoring for drift or distortion.

    None   Some   Reasonable   Good   High   Very high

52. *Work measurement*
    Knowledge of work measurement techniques for both direct and indirect work, and their application in the construction of a wage payment system.

    None   Some   Reasonable   Good   High   Very high

53. *Motivational schemes:*
    Ability to construct a pay system based on motivation/performance for direct blue collar employees.

    None   Some   Reasonable   Good   High   Very high

54. Ability to construct a pay system based on motivation/performance for indirect blue collar, administrative and technical staff.

    None   Some   Reasonable   Good   High   Very high

55. Ability to construct a pay system based on motivation/performance for managerial staff.

    None   Some   Reasonable   Good   High   Very high

56. Ability to construct a pay system based on motivation/performance for sales and marketing staff.

    None   Some   Reasonable   Good   High   Very high

57. *Major changes*
    Experience of proposing/implementing a major change in a remuneration system for a major grouping of personnel.

    None   Some   Reasonable   Good   High   Very high

58. *Monitoring systems*
    Ability to monitor payment systems to identify drifts, distortion, anomalies and manipulation.

    None   Some   Reasonable   Good   High   Very high

Health and Safety

59. *Legislation*
    Working knowledge of the Health and Safety at Work Act, Factories Act, and statutory regulations.

    None   Some   Reasonable   Good   High   Very high

60. *Legal decisions*
    Up-to-date knowledge of legal decisions and the ability to interpret their significance for the organisation.

    None   Some   Reasonable   Good   High   Very high

61. *Chairing a committee*
    Ability to chair successfully and effectively a health and safety committee consisting of both employee representatives and line management.

    None   Some   Reasonable   Good   High   Very high

62. *Health and safety programmes*
    Experience of constructing a health and safety programme which is fully understood and supported at all levels throughout the organisation and of ensuring its systems and procedures are regularly monitored for effectiveness.

    None   Some   Reasonable   Good   High   Very high

63. *Medical facilities*
    Ability to ensure occupational health facilities provide both treatment and preventive medicine and offer guidance in reducing mental and physical stress.

    None   Some   Reasonable   Good   High   Very high

Employee Services, Benefits and Welfare

Experience of administering within agreed budgets and monitoring for deviation from those budgets in the following schemes:

64. *Company car scheme*

    None   Some   Reasonable   Good   High   Very high

65. *Pension scheme*

    None   Some   Reasonable   Good   High   Very high

66. *Sickness payment scheme*

    None   Some   Reasonable   Good   High   Very high

67. *Subsidised catering*

    None   Some   Reasonable   Good   High   Very high

68. *Sport and social facilities*

    None   Some   Reasonable   Good   High   Very high

69. *Service and retirement recognition*

    None   Some   Reasonable   Good   High   Very high

FUNCTIONAL SKILLS PROFILE C9
PURCHASING ▶

Preamble

Listed below is a range of the skills involved in purchasing. The questionnaire is obviously designed for managers who have specialist skills in purchasing. Even with such managers the skill levels vary considerably across the range and over time.

Please read the list and consider it. Then ring the level of skill you feel that you have at present in each area. The broad comparison is with the skills needed as 'head of Purchasing' in, say,

- a medium-sized business of, say, £20m to £30m turnover or around 1,000 employees;
- an NHS unit, for example, a hospital;
- a District Council of, say, 100,000 population.

One would expect a capable and experienced senior manager to have a varying level of these skills depending on managerial level, past training, and experience.

There is inevitably some overlap in many of the areas and room for some difference of view about definitions. The objective is to arrive at a reasonable overall self-assessment for your own use.

The ratings are as follows:

None No significant level of skill and/or knowledge.

Some Some knowledge and/or skill but lower than you would prefer.

Reasonable Reasonable level of knowledge and/or skill enabling you to cope in that area without major difficulties.

Good Good level of knowledge and/or skill enabling you to cope more than adequately. Probably about average for a senior manager in a medium-sized business.

High High skill and/or knowledge level such as to encourage you to feel rather pleased with your performance.

Very high   Very high skill and/or knowledge level. You regard yourself as outstanding and your colleagues sometimes comment favourably.

The areas are subdivided and are not listed in order of importance.

Corporate Emphasis

1. *Purchasing to sales ratio*
   Knowledge and appreciation of the significance of the proportion of total sales revenue being expended by purchasing.

   None   Some   Reasonable   Good   High   Very high

2. *Value for money*
   Ability to implement policies and strategies to ensure maximum value is obtained for every pound expended.

   None   Some   Reasonable   Good   High   Very high

3. *Contribution to profits*
   Knowledge, appreciation, and the ability to communicate authoritatively, the unique potential of purchasing's contribution to profits.

   None   Some   Reasonable   Good   High   Very high

4. *Inventory control*
   Ability to exercise strong influence in the control of company inventories.

   None   Some   Reasonable   Good   High   Very high

5. *Reciprocal trading*
   Ability to exercise discretion in optimising reciprocal trading with customers and suppliers.

   None   Some   Reasonable   Good   High   Very high

6. *Fair dealing*
   Ability to establish and maintain the company's reputation for fair dealing, while ensuring the benefits to the company accrue from hard-bargaining.

   None   Some   Reasonable   Good   High   Very high

7. *Inducements*
   Ability to establish and maintain very high standards of conduct in connection with every form of potential inducement at all levels.

   None   Some   Reasonable   Good   High   Very high

8. *Supplier 'partnership'*
Ability to create and maintain a consensus of the concept of 'partnership' with main suppliers – without prejudicing purchasing's sovereignty.

None   Some   Reasonable   Good   High   Very high

Procurement

9. *Enquiring*
Knowledge, understanding, and experience of conducting optimum enquiry campaigns, ie obtaining adequate spread of appropriate competitive bids, while avoiding the uneconomical use of resources upon inappropriate alternatives.

None   Some   Reasonable   Good   High   Very high

10. *Bid-analysis*
Ability to analyse, and take decisions upon suppliers' bids to ensure maximum benefit to the company.

None   Some   Reasonable   Good   High   Very high

11. *Ordering*
Ability to draft purchase orders and contract documents clearly, concisely, and without ambiguity.

None   Some   Reasonable   Good   High   Very high

12. *Expediting*
    Knowledge and experience of establishing and maintaining expediting systems, together with imagination and flair for conducting special expediting campaigns in emergencies.

    None   Some   Reasonable   Good   High   Very high

13. *Setting priorities*
    Possession of a strong capacity for determining priorities in the overall best interests of the company when presented with limited options.

    None   Some   Reasonable   Good   High   Very high

14. *Payment of accounts*
    Knowledge and understanding of the effects upon suppliers of non-payment of suppliers' accounts, with an ability to make judgements on these, and to be effective in obtaining payment as necessary through accounts.

    None   Some   Reasonable   Good   High   Very high

15. *Goods receiving*
    Ability to establish and maintain effective systems in connection with prompt reporting of goods and services received, and the satisfactory integration of quality control and inspection procedures.

    None   Some   Reasonable   Good   High   Very high

Commercial

16. *Price negotiation*
    Ability to negotiate the most favourable prices possible along with preferred terms of payment while avoiding the reputation for creating 'Dutch Auctions'.

    None   Some   Reasonable   Good   High   Very high

17. *Delivery negotiation*
    Ability to negotiate the best (realistic) delivery commitments, with appropriate penalty clauses (without premiums where possible) when time is of the essence.

    None   Some   Reasonable   Good   High   Very high

18. *Re-negotiation*
    Ability to re-negotiate more favourable prices and deliveries whenever circumstances develop which offer such opportunities.

    None   Some   Reasonable   Good   High   Very high

19. *Foreign currency deals*
    Possession of a thorough understanding of the ramifications of purchasing from abroad vis-à-vis foreign currency dealings, with an ability to liaise with finance department in these transactions.

    None   Some   Reasonable   Good   High   Very high

Contractual

20. *Contract drafting*
    Knowledge, understanding and experience of the drafting of practical, commercial contracts; also the ability to ensure legal accuracy throughout the offer, acceptance, and acknowledgement phases of contracts.

    None   Some   Reasonable   Good   High   Very high

21. *Commercial law*
    Familiarity with commercial legislation, especially with its proliferation in recent years.

    None   Some   Reasonable   Good   High   Very high

Source Marketing

22. *Potential new sources of supply*
    Knowledge of potential sources of supply worldwide, and an appreciation of their competitive status compared with current suppliers.

    None   Some   Reasonable   Good   High   Very high

23. *Personal adaptability and mobility*
    Ability to travel worldwide at short notice, and to cope with all the challenges which present themselves on overseas missions.

    None   Some   Reasonable   Good   High   Very high

24. *Manufacturing processes*
    Possession of a sound working knowledge of the up-to-date manufacturing processes involved in producing the required materials.

    None   Some   Reasonable   Good   High   Very high

25. *Quality control*
    Ability to work closely with quality control in carrying out vendor rating exercises on current as well as new suppliers.

    None   Some   Reasonable   Good   High   Very high

26. *Suppliers' financial status*
    Ability to interpret suppliers' balance sheets in the context of their financial stability.

    None   Some   Reasonable   Good   High   Very high

27. *Purchasing's role in the VA team*
    Knowledge and experience of the involvement of purchasing in value analysis studies.

    None   Some   Reasonable   Good   High   Very high

28. *Linking designers with suppliers*
    Ability to bring together suppliers' expertise with company designers, to co-operate in deciding upon the most effective options.

    None   Some   Reasonable   Good   High   Very high

Capital Plant and Equipment Acquisitions

29. *Acquisition agent*
    Ability to work closely and effectively with specialist user-departments in the efficient procurement of all capital plant and equipment.

    None   Some   Reasonable   Good   High   Very high

30. *Holding the purse strings*
    Ability to ensure that user-departments do not prejudice the company's best interests by making unilateral or unauthorised commitments with suppliers.

    None   Some   Reasonable   Good   High   Very high

31. *Commercial integrity*
    Experience in maintaining confidentiality and security of suppliers' tenders throughout multi-function negotiations.

    None   Some   Reasonable   Good   High   Very high

32. *Expenditure 'long-stop'*
    Ability to exercise proper authority across the company in the prevention of any serious violation of company procedures in connection with the expenditure of moneys on capital equipment.

    None   Some   Reasonable   Good   High   Very high

Disposal of Company Assets and Scrap Materials

33. *Good commercial practices*
    Ability to establish and maintain good commercial practices in the sale of company assets and scrap materials.

    None   Some   Reasonable   Good   High   Very high

34. *Keeper of the company 'silver'*
    Ability to establish and maintain strict company procedures for the correct authorisation of the disposal of company assets, and the ability to adhere rigidly to these procedures.

    None   Some   Reasonable   Good   High   Very high

35. *Scrupulous dealing with the 'unscrupulous'*
    Appreciation of the special hazards which can obtain in the dealings with second-hand plant and materials, and the importance of scrupulous behaviour in these transactions.

    None   Some   Reasonable   Good   High   Very high

The Effects of National and International Events on Supplies

36. *Current affairs*
    Knowledge and understanding of current affairs at home and abroad likely to affect availability of materials and/or their prices.

    None   Some   Reasonable   Good   High   Very high

Company Takeovers, Mergers, Failures, and Appointments

37. *Company changes*
    Knowledge and understanding of the likely effects of company changes which could be of concern when these are suppliers.

    None   Some   Reasonable   Good   High   Very high

38. *Executive changes*
    Knowledge and understanding of the changes which might take place following the announcement of executive appointments in suppliers' companies.

    None   Some   Reasonable   Good   High   Very high

New Technology

39. *Business systems*
    Knowledge of technological developments in business systems, and an ability to assess their benefits, or otherwise, to the purchasing function.

    None   Some   Reasonable   Good   High   Very high

Staff Development

40. *Staff training*
    Ability to ensure the ongoing development of purchasing staff, by on-the-job experience, as well as outside courses.

    None   Some   Reasonable   Good   High   Very high

41. *Staff promotion*
    Ability to prepare, in a systematic manner, staff for promotion and higher responsibility.

    None   Some   Reasonable   Good   High   Very high

Measurement of Purchasing Performance

42. *Practical monitoring*
    Knowledge and understanding of the application of basic practical criteria for monitoring the performance of purchasing, without the unwieldy involvement of over-sophisticated techniques.

    None   Some   Reasonable   Good   High   Very high

FUNCTIONAL SKILLS PROFILE C10
EXPORTING ▶

Preamble

Listed below is a range of the skills involved in export marketing and sales. The questionnaire is obviously designed for managers who have specialist skills in export marketing and sales. Even with such managers the skill levels vary considerably across the range and over time.

We define exporting as the ability to manage the penetration of existing and potential export markets in your organisation's business area, including marketing, selling and administration. This profile should be used in conjunction with the more general Functional Skills Profile C6: Marketing and Sales.

Please read the list and consider it. Then ring the level of skill you feel that you have at present in each area. The broad comparison is with the skills needed as 'head of Export' in a medium-sized business of, say, £20m to £30m turnover or around 1,000 employees.

One would expect a capable and experienced senior manager to have a varying level of these skills depending on managerial level, past training, and experience.

There is inevitably some overlap in many of the areas and room for some difference of view about definitions. The objective is to arrive at a reasonable overall self-assessment for your own use.

The ratings are as follows:

None　　　No significant level of skill and/or knowledge.

Some　　　Some knowledge and/or skill but lower than you would prefer.

Reasonable　　Reasonable level of knowledge and/or skill enabling you to cope in that area without major difficulties.

Good　　　Good level of knowledge and/or skill enabling you to cope more than adequately. Probably about average for a senior manager in a medium-sized business.

High High skill and/or knowledge level such as to encourage you to feel rather pleased with your performance.

Very high Very high skill and/or knowledge level. You regard yourself as outstanding and your colleagues sometimes comment favourably.

The areas are subdivided and are not listed in order of importance.

Market Research and Selection

1. *New markets*
   Skill or experience in conducting market surveys in new markets for an existing product sold elsewhere.

   None   Some   Reasonable   Good   High   Very high

2. *New products*
   Skill or experience in conducting market research for a new product in an existing market.

   None   Some   Reasonable   Good   High   Very high

3. *New products and new markets*
   Experience in conducting market research for a totally new product in a totally new market.

   None   Some   Reasonable   Good   High   Very high

4. *Cultural and related factors*
   Awareness of the cultural, social or religious factors affecting product acceptability in an overseas market.

   None   Some   Reasonable   Good   High   Very high

5. *Collecting data*
   Skill or experience in collecting marketing information or advice from UK government agencies, international trade associations, banks, overseas agents.

   None   Some   Reasonable   Good   High   Very high

6. *Marketing trips*
   Skill or experience in planning and conducting overseas marketing trips.

   None   Some   Reasonable   Good   High   Very high

7. *Statistical analysis*
   Skill or experience in using statistical techniques in order to analyse data and information.

   None   Some   Reasonable   Good   High   Very high

8. *Determining mix*
   Skill or experience in determining the appropriate marketing mix for each overseas market.

   None   Some   Reasonable   Good   High   Very high

Legal and Ethical Constraints on Overseas Trading

9. *Trade restrictions*
   Awareness of UK government or trade association restrictions on the sale of particular goods to particular countries.

   None   Some   Reasonable   Good   High   Very high

10. *Legal constraints*
    Awareness of legal constraints in the overseas market which will adversely affect sales opportunities there, including import duties and licences, quotas, technical standards.

    None   Some   Reasonable   Good   High   Very high

11. *Standards of behaviour*
    Ability to conform to your company's moral standards, and ensure government legalities are adhered to while at the same time customs or cultural expectations are met in the overseas market.

    None   Some   Reasonable   Good   High   Very high

12. *Cutting red tape*
    Skill or experience in overcoming bureaucratic hurdles which obstruct or delay the passage of goods.

    None   Some   Reasonable   Good   High   Very high

Principles of Law in Overseas Trade

13. *Contract law*
    Knowledge of the law of contract including awareness of the features, conditions and terms necessary to make a valid contract.

    None   Some   Reasonable   Good   High   Very high

14. *Factors in contracts*
    Awareness of the factors affecting contractual obligations including misrepresentation, discharge of contract by repudiation or frustration, and remedies for breach of contract.

    None   Some   Reasonable   Good   High   Very high

15. *Sale of Goods Acts*
    Knowledge of the Sale of Goods Acts particularly as applies to international trading.

    None   Some   Reasonable   Good   High   Very high

16. *Cross-border legal standing*
    Awareness of the contract law appertaining in any particular market in which your company trades, including its legal standing in the UK and also the validity of UK and EC law in that market.

    None   Some   Reasonable   Good   High   Very high

17. *Competition law*
    Awareness of the varieties of competition law which prevail in overseas markets.

    None   Some   Reasonable   Good   High   Very high

18. *Law and finance*
    Extent of understanding of the legal aspects in financing exports, including bills of exchange, letters of credit and other forms of payment.

    None   Some   Reasonable   Good   High   Very high

Overseas Trade and Payments

19. *International framework*
    Knowledge of the international financial framework within which overseas trading occurs, including commodity markets, balance of payments issues, gross domestic product of overseas markets.

    None   Some   Reasonable   Good   High   Very high

20. *Trade organisations*
    Knowledge of the international financial trade organisations including IMF, GATT, EC and COMECON.

    None   Some   Reasonable   Good   High   Very high

21. *Eastern Europe*
    Awareness of the difficulties in trading with evolving economies in Eastern European countries including currency balancing, barter and bilateral trade.

    None   Some   Reasonable   Good   High   Very high

22. *Terms of sale*
    Knowledge of the wide variety of terms of sale including FOB, CIF, FIS, FOR/FOT, C&F.

    None   Some   Reasonable   Good   High   Very high

23. *Bills of exchange*
    Knowledge of the advantages and complications of using bills of exchange.

    None   Some   Reasonable   Good   High   Very high

24. *Credit information*
    Skill or experience in obtaining credit intelligence on potential customers.

    None   Some   Reasonable   Good   High   Very high

25. *Credit insurance*
    Knowledge of the wide variety of insuring credit risk cover including use of ECGD, letters of credit and use of export houses and factoring companies.

    None   Some   Reasonable   Good   High   Very high

26. *Alternative finance*
    Knowledge of the wide variety of alternative sources of bank finance including promissory notes, open accounts schemes, post shipment finance.

    None   Some   Reasonable   Good   High   Very high

27. *Other trading methods*
    Awareness of other trading methods including royalty agreements, licensing, joint ventures and consignment trading.

    None   Some   Reasonable   Good   High   Very high

28. *Export insurance*
    Knowledge of the wide varieties of export insurance schemes including the use of insurance companies and brokers.

    None   Some   Reasonable   Good   High   Very high

29. *Foreign exchange*
    Awareness of the risks associated with fluctuations in the foreign exchange market and skill in planning for these.

    None   Some   Reasonable   Good   High   Very high

Documentation

30. *Export documentation*
    Knowledge of the wide variety of documentation associated with exports including consignment notes, certificates of origin, bills of lading, insurance documents and those associated with passing title of goods.

    None   Some   Reasonable   Good   High   Very high

31. *Customs requirements*
    Level of understanding of documentation required to conform to customs obligations including the Harmonised Commodity Description and Coding System (HS), the Integrated Customs Tariff (TARIC), etc.

    None   Some   Reasonable   Good   High   Very high

32. *Correct marking and packaging*
    Level of knowledge and understanding of need for obligatory forms of marking and packing, which conform to UK customs requirements and regulations in the particular overseas market.

    None   Some   Reasonable   Good   High   Very high

Distribution

33. *Costs and physical difficulties*
    Skill and experience in determining the costs and physical distribution difficulties of trading overseas.

    None   Some   Reasonable   Good   High   Very high

34. *Effective channels*
    Skill and experience in selecting the most appropriate and cost-effective channel of distribution including agents, distributors and specialist outlets.

    None   Some   Reasonable   Good   High   Very high

35. *Negotiating with handlers*
    Ability to negotiate the best possible terms with cargo handlers and shipping agents for sea, air or vehicle distribution.

    None   Some   Reasonable   Good   High   Very high

36. *Assembled v kit format*
   Knowledge of the difficulties or advantages associated with exporting in a fully assembled form or in a kit format for assembly in the overseas market.

   None   Some   Reasonable   Good   High   Very high

37. *Small items*
   Experience in using postal and courier services for small items.

   None   Some   Reasonable   Good   High   Very high

Communications

38. *Written communication*
   Awareness of the need for clear, concise and simple written communication including telefax and telex, particularly for overseas markets where verbal communication is impractical or difficult.

   None   Some   Reasonable   Good   High   Very high

39. *Foreign languages*
   Ability to use other languages for a common form of communication where English is not possible, for example, French and Spanish.

   None   Some   Reasonable   Good   High   Very high

40. *Technical translation*
    Awareness of the difficulties associated with technical translation and the means to overcome these.

    None   Some   Reasonable   Good   High   Very high

Risk

41. *Levels of risk*
    Skill or experience in determining the level of risk associated with exporting a particular product to a particular overseas market in relation to:

    a) Securing payment

    None   Some   Reasonable   Good   High   Very high

    b) Assuring the avoidance of diversion of goods

    None   Some   Reasonable   Good   High   Very high

    c) Determining when to manufacture products in relation to the time taken to secure export credit guarantees

    None   Some   Reasonable   Good   High   Very high

d) Determining when to ship or release to the customer or agent

None   Some   Reasonable   Good   High   Very high

Service

42. *Factors affecting export service*
    Implications for export service in your company of product manufacturing time, product life cycle and quality standards.

    None   Some   Reasonable   Good   High   Very high

43. *After-sales service*
    Skill or experience in determining the level and type of after-sales service for a particular overseas market.

    None   Some   Reasonable   Good   High   Very high

44. *Parts availability*
    Skill or experience in determining the level of parts requirements by reference to the nature of product usage in a particular market.

    None   Some   Reasonable   Good   High   Very high

Management and Resourcing

45. *Appointing overseas resources*
    Skill or experience in appointing agents, wholesalers, specialist outlets or local national representatives in an overseas market.

    None   Some   Reasonable   Good   High   Very high

46. *Controlling overseas resources*
    Skill or experience in instituting the appropriate type and level of controls to ensure quality of service and performance by agents, distributors, etc.

    None   Some   Reasonable   Good   High   Very high

47. *Managing the shipping office*
    Ability to manage the shipping office at your UK base.

    None   Some   Reasonable   Good   High   Very high

48. *Managing UK nationals overseas*
    Skill or experience in managing UK national representatives in overseas markets, together with ensuring their proper motivation and reward.

    None   Some   Reasonable   Good   High   Very high

49. *Budgets and control*
    Ability to prepare budgets for the international sales and marketing function in your company and to measure actual performance against these.

    None   Some   Reasonable   Good   High   Very high

50. *Formulating policy*
    Ability to prepare an overall company policy on overseas trading with regard to product mix, promotion needs, pricing and distribution.

    None   Some   Reasonable   Good   High   Very high

FUNCTIONAL SKILLS PROFILE C11
INFORMATION TECHNOLOGY ▶

Preamble

Listed below is a range of the skills involved in information technology. The questionnaire is obviously designed for managers who have specialist skills in information technology. Even with such managers the skill levels vary considerably across the range and over time.

Please read the list and consider it. Then ring the level of skill you feel that you have at present in each area. The broad comparison is with the skills needed as 'head of Information Technology' in, say,

- a medium-sized business of, say, £20m to £30m turnover or around 1,000 employees;
- an NHS unit, for example, a hospital;
- a District Council of, say, 100,000 population.

One would expect a capable and experienced senior manager to have a varying level of these skills depending on managerial level, past training, and experience.

There is inevitably some overlap in many of the areas and room for some difference of view about definitions. The objective is to arrive at a reasonable overall self-assessment for your own use.

The ratings are as follows:

None   No significant level of skill and/or knowledge.

Some   Some knowledge and/or skill but lower than you would prefer.

Reasonable   Reasonable level of knowledge and/or skill enabling you to cope in that area without major difficulties.

Good   Good level of knowledge and/or skill enabling you to cope more than adequately. Probably about average for a senior manager in a medium-sized business.

High High skill and/or knowledge level such as to encourage you to feel rather pleased with your performance.

Very high Very high skill and/or knowledge level. You regard yourself as outstanding and your colleagues sometimes comment favourably.

The areas are subdivided and are not listed in order of importance.

Knowledge

1. *Hardware – mainframe*
   Up-to-date knowledge of mainframe computer types and capabilities.

   None   Some   Reasonable   Good   High   Very high

2. *Hardware – mini*
   Up-to-date knowledge of minicomputer types and capabilities.

   None   Some   Reasonable   Good   High   Very high

3. *Hardware – micro*
   Up-to-date knowledge of microcomputer types and capabilities.

   None   Some   Reasonable   Good   High   Very high

4. *Telecommunications*
   Up-to-date knowledge of telecommunications systems in relation to computers.

   None   Some   Reasonable   Good   High   Very high

5. *Software – operating systems*
   Up-to-date knowledge of software – operating systems.

   None   Some   Reasonable   Good   High   Very high

6. *Software – database management systems*
   Up-to-date knowledge of database management systems.

   None   Some   Reasonable   Good   High   Very high

7. *Software – data dictionaries*
   Up-to-date knowledge of data dictionaries.

   None   Some   Reasonable   Good   High   Very high

8. *Software – application generators/4 GLs*
   Up-to-date knowledge of application generators/4 GLs.

   None   Some   Reasonable   Good   High   Very high

9. *Software – query languages*
   Up-to-date knowledge of query languages.

   None   Some   Reasonable   Good   High   Very high

10. *Application – packages*
    Up-to-date knowledge of packages available.

    None   Some   Reasonable   Good   High   Very high

11. *Application – office automation*
    Up-to-date knowledge of office automation.

    None   Some   Reasonable   Good   High   Very high

12. *Application – information centre*
    Up-to-date knowledge of the information centre concept.

    None   Some   Reasonable   Good   High   Very high

13. *Systems development – structured analysis techniques*
    Up-to-date knowledge of structured analysis techniques.

    None   Some   Reasonable   Good   High   Very high

14. *Systems development – project evaluation and control*
    Up-to-date knowledge of project evaluation and control.

    None   Some   Reasonable   Good   High   Very high

15. *Systems development – standards*
    Up-to-date knowledge of standards.

    None   Some   Reasonable   Good   High   Very high

16. *Systems development – contract staff/software house*
    Up-to-date knowledge of selecting and controlling contract staff/software house.

    None   Some   Reasonable   Good   High   Very high

Direction

17. *Goals*
    Ability to set appropriate goals for the use of data processing within the company and obtain management understanding and agreement to them.

    None   Some   Reasonable   Good   High   Very high

18. *Plans*
    Ability to develop meaningful data processing plans taking into account current DP capabilities, current and future needs, trends in technology, and gain management's approval and support.

    None   Some   Reasonable   Good   High   Very high

19. *Communication*
    Ability to communicate with users and top management in order to appreciate their perspectives and increase their awareness of data processing technical issues.

    None   Some   Reasonable   Good   High   Very high

20. *Involvement*
    Ability to obtain senior management's involvement in, and understanding of, their role in the application of data processing within the business.

    None   Some   Reasonable   Good   High   Very high

Resources

21. *Skills assessment*
    Ability to assess the skills needed within the data processing department, identify shortfalls, and justify recruitment.

    None   Some   Reasonable   Good   High   Very high

22. *Recruit*
    Ability to recruit the appropriate skills, at the appropriate remuneration package.

    None   Some   Reasonable   Good   High   Very high

23. *Retain and train*
    Ability to retain and train data processing staff by designing proper training programmes and providing career development.

    None   Some   Reasonable   Good   High   Very high

24. *Strategy*
    Ability to establish short and medium-term resource plans within a long-term hardware strategy.

    None   Some   Reasonable   Good   High   Very high

25. *Selection*
    Ability to evaluate and select hardware and software within the context of a medium-term technical resources plan.

    None   Some   Reasonable   Good   High   Very high

26. *Budgeting*
    Ability to budget for data processing resources, monitor expenditure and account for deviations.

    None   Some   Reasonable   Good   High   Very high

27. *Justification*
    Ability to establish a justification process for expenditure on data processing.

    None   Some   Reasonable   Good   High   Very high

Effectiveness and Efficiency

28. *Systems development environment*
    Ability to provide a systems development which gives high user satisfaction, uses good standards for improving effectiveness, and which considers alternatives to in-house development.

    None   Some   Reasonable   Good   High   Very high

29. *Systems maintenance*
    Ability to provide a systems maintenance function which includes user participation and gives a good cost/benefit service.

    None   Some   Reasonable   Good   High   Very high

30. *Standards*
    Ability to establish and maintain good standards for the development, hand-over to production, and maintenance of systems.

    None   Some   Reasonable   Good   High   Very high

31. *Cost-effectiveness*
    Ability to establish a cost-effective system of reporting costs to users; for systems development, production, maintenance and general support.

    None   Some   Reasonable   Good   High   Very high

32. *Quality control*
    Ability to establish and maintain a high quality data processing facility with good levels of service, efficiently run and operated at a cost consistent with user demands.

    None   Some   Reasonable   Good   High   Very high

33. *Data communications*
    Ability to establish and maintain a high quality data communications facility within the context of a network strategy which provides all levels of users with facilities consistent with their needs.

    None   Some   Reasonable   Good   High   Very high

34. *Facilities*
    Ability to provide the facilities for users to obtain access to required data within the constraints of time, costs, and access rights.

    None   Some   Reasonable   Good   High   Very high

35. *End-user satisfaction*
    Ability to provide a level of end-user computing consistent with the maturity of users, resources used, needs, costs, and level of protection required for programs and data.

    None   Some   Reasonable   Good   High   Very high

36. *Reviewing new technology*
    Ability to focus and control effort spent on reviewing new technology given its consistency with the goals for data processing within the organisation.

    None   Some   Reasonable   Good   High   Very high

Control and Accomplishment

37. *Planning*
    Ability to establish an overall Data Processing plan of which senior management is aware, and control its implementation with good levels of communication both within and outside the data processing function.

    None   Some   Reasonable   Good   High   Very high

38. *Quality control*
    Ability to maintain at high quality the work produced by the Data Processing function as evidenced by end-user satisfaction.

    None   Some   Reasonable   Good   High   Very high

39. *Security*
    Ability to establish a high level of data processing security covering all computer resources with good levels of control both inside and outside the data processing function.

    None   Some   Reasonable   Good   High   Very high

40. *Dependency assessment*
    Ability to assess the level of dependency on critical applications and develop a disaster recovery plan consistent with the perceived risks and costs.

    None   Some   Reasonable   Good   High   Very high

41. *Critical target assessment*
    Ability to assess the critical targets for data processing within the organisation, to achieve the necessary results and to communicate the accomplishments of data processing to senior management.

    None   Some   Reasonable   Good   High   Very high

42. *User expectations management*
Ability to manage users' expectations consistent with their understanding, their awareness, and of the resources and costs involved; actively plan for user satisfaction within all the different areas of the data processing function.

None   Some   Reasonable   Good   High   Very high

FUNCTIONAL SKILLS PROFILE C12
NEW TECHNOLOGY ▶

Preamble

Listed below is a range of new technology skills which are relevant to a wide range of management appointments. None of us have all these skills, and our skill levels vary considerably across the range and over time, and reflect the industry, products and services with which we have been associated. For the purpose of this questionnaire, new technology is defined as 'the application of scientific research and development which radically changes and improves the ability of an organisation to carry out its activities'.

Please read the list and consider it, then tick or ring the level of skill you feel that you have at present in each area. The broad comparison is with the skills needed as 'head of New Technology' in, say,

- a medium-sized business of, say, £20m to £30m turnover or around 1,000 employees;
- an NHS unit, for example, a hospital;
- a District Council of, say, 100,000 population.

One would expect a capable and experienced senior manager to have a varying level of these skills depending on managerial level, past training, and experience. There is inevitably some overlap in the areas and room for some difference of view about definitions. The objective is to arrive at a reasonable overall self-assessment for your own use.

The ratings are as follows:

None No significant level of skill and/or knowledge.

Some Some knowledge and/or skill but lower than you would prefer.

Reasonable Reasonable level of knowledge and/or skill enabling you to cope in that area without major difficulties.

Good Good level of knowledge and/or skill enabling you to

| | High | High skill and/or knowledge level such as to encourage you to feel rather pleased with your performance. |

cope more than adequately. Probably about average for a senior manager in a medium-sized business.

High High skill and/or knowledge level such as to encourage you to feel rather pleased with your performance.

Very high Very high skill and/or knowledge level. You regard yourself as outstanding and your colleagues sometimes comment favourably.

The areas are subdivided and are not listed in order of importance.

General Areas

Almost every business is subject to the emergence of new technology in the following general areas. Please identify level of experience or knowledge/understanding of new technological developments in each area.

	None	*Some*	*Reasonable*	*Good*	*High*	*Very high*
1. *Transport*						
2. *Packaging*						
3. *Information processing* a) *Mainframe*						
b) *Micro/PC*						
4. *Communications*						
5. *Health and safety*						
6. *Sales and marketing*						

	None	Some	Reasonable	Good	High	Very high
7. Energy, heating and ventilation						
8. Building construction						
9. Printing						
10. Administration, including automated office systems						

Specific Areas

The following areas are more specific to each company or business. Please indicate the level of experience or knowledge/understanding of new technology in each area as it applies to your company at present.

	None	Some	Reasonable	Good	High	Very high
11. Research and development, including materials						
12. Manufacture/processing, including CIM, FMS, robotics, automation and bio-engineering						
13. Control and instrumentation						

	None	Some	Reasonable	Good	High	Very high
14. Design, including CAD/CAM						
15. Quality, including test and inspection						
16. Production engineering						

Other Functional Areas

Please indicate your acquaintance with the extent to which new technology is being utilised in the following functional areas of your company.

	None	Some	Reasonable	Good	High	Very high
17. Sales and marketing						
18. Finance						
19. Research and development						
20. Design						
21. Applications engineering						
22. Production engineering						

	None	Some	Reasonable	Good	High	Very high
23. Manufacturing/ processing						
24. Purchasing						
25. Export						
26. Data processing						
27. Personnel and employee relations						
28. Warehousing and stock control						
29. Stock and material movement						
30. Point of sale						

Technology Transfer

31. *Applied research*
    Knowledge or experience of the development of applied research in universities and research centres.

    None   Some   Reasonable   Good   High   Very high

32. *Technology transfer*
    Experience of technology transfer from universities, research centres, science parks, innovation centres.

    None   Some   Reasonable   Good   High   Very high

33. *Corporate objectives*
    Skill in relating an R&D/new technology project to overall corporate objectives.

    None   Some   Reasonable   Good   High   Very high

34. *Project management*
    Experience of managing a research and development project on any area of new technology.

    None   Some   Reasonable   Good   High   Very high

35. *By-products*
    Experience of managing the development in your own company of by-products, including skills and services arising from mainstream activities.

    None   Some   Reasonable   Good   High   Very high

36. *External promotion*
    Experience of promoting, marketing or selling your company's new technology developments to other organisations.

    None   Some   Reasonable   Good   High   Very high

37. *Intellectual property*
    Experience of controlling intellectual property protection for new technology developed within your own company.

    None   Some   Reasonable   Good   High   Very high

Keeping Up To Date

38. *Keeping abreast*
    Level of skill in keeping yourself abreast of developments in new technology as can be related to your area of responsibility.

    None   Some   Reasonable   Good   High   Very high

39. *Staff communication*
    Level of skill and experience in keeping your staff informed of new technological developments which could affect the way they carry out their jobs.

    None   Some   Reasonable   Good   High   Very high

40. *Staff development*
Level of experience or knowledge in ensuring your staff are trained and developed to maximise the use of available new technology.

None   Some   Reasonable   Good   High   Very high

Introducing New Technology

41. *Evaluation*
Skill or experience in evaluating new technology and comparing it with existing methods.

None   Some   Reasonable   Good   High   Very high

42. *Capital proposals*
Ability to construct a capital expenditure proposal which justifies the introduction of an aspect of new technology.

None   Some   Reasonable   Good   High   Very high

43. *Working practices*
Appreciation or experience of identifying changes in working practices required to ensure the successful introduction of new technology.

None   Some   Reasonable   Good   High   Very high

44. *Impact on people*
    Ability or experience in determining the impact on people of introducing new technology and its related new working practices.

    None   Some   Reasonable   Good   High   Very high

45. *Negotiation*
    Skill or experience in negotiating the introduction of new technology with staff, including trade unions.

    None   Some   Reasonable   Good   High   Very high

46. *Budgetary control*
    Skill or experience in maintaining budgetary control during the early phases of new technology and until it is regarded as longer-term practice.

    None   Some   Reasonable   Good   High   Very high

New Technology Outside Your Company

47. *Competitors*
    Skill or experience in gaining knowledge of competitors' use and benefit of new technology not currently used in your own company.

    None   Some   Reasonable   Good   High   Very high

48. *Suppliers*
    Skill or experience in determining new technology used by your suppliers which may have an effect on your own company in carrying out its activities in the most efficient manner.

    None   Some   Reasonable   Good   High   Very high

49. *Customers*
    Skill or experience in determining your customers' use of new technology which may affect the quality of the product they expect from your company or which may require some change in your own methods of working.

    None   Some   Reasonable   Good   High   Very high

FUNCTIONAL SKILLS PROFILE C13
RETAILING, WAREHOUSING AND DISTRIBUTION ▶

Preamble

Listed below is a range of skills involved in retailing, warehousing and distribution. The questionnaire is obviously designed for managers who have specialist skills in retailing, warehousing and distribution. Even with such managers the skill levels vary considerably across the range and over time. Please read the list and consider it. Then ring the level of skill you feel that you have at present in each area. The broad comparison is with the skills needed as 'head of Retailing, Warehousing and Distribution' in, say,

- a medium-sized business of, say, £20m to £30m turnover or around 1,000 employees;
- an NHS unit, for example, a hospital;
- a District Council of, say, 100,000 population.

One would expect a capable and experienced senior manager to have a varying level of these skills depending on managerial level, past training, and experience. There is inevitably some overlap in many of the areas and room for some difference of view about definitions. The objective is to arrive at a reasonable overall self-assessment for your own use.

The ratings are as follows:

None   No significant level of skill and/or knowledge.

Some   Some knowledge and/or skill but lower than you would prefer.

Reasonable Reasonable level of knowledge and/or skill enabling you to cope in that area without major difficulties.

Good   Good level of knowledge and/or skill enabling you to cope more than adequately. Probably about average for a senior manager in a medium-sized business.

High   High skill and/or knowledge level such as to encourage you to feel rather pleased with your performance.

Very high   Very high skill and/or knowledge level. You regard yourself as outstanding and your colleagues sometimes comment favourably.

The areas are subdivided and are not listed in order of importance.

Planning for Distribution

1. *Strategy*
   An understanding of the key aspects in planning a distribution strategy, in particular the factors influencing:

   - choice of channels;
   - decision on one channel or several;
   - decision to go direct to customer or through intermediaries;
   - decision on amount of expenditure on distribution;
   - taking a complete or partial financial interest in available channels.

   None   Some   Reasonable   Good   High   Very high

2. *Total cost approach to distribution (TCD)*

   None   Some   Reasonable   Good   High   Very high

Distribution Channels

3. *The wholesaler*
   Knowledge of the structure of the wholesale trade in the UK and the factors influencing a decision to distribute through it.

   None   Some   Reasonable   Good   High   Very high

4. *Independent retailers*
   Knowledge of the structure of the independent retail sector, its advantages and disadvantages as a channel of distribution.

   None   Some   Reasonable   Good   High   Very high

5. *Voluntary groups*
   Knowledge of the structure of voluntary groups of independent retailers and of the advantages and disadvantages of using them as a channel of distribution.

   None   Some   Reasonable   Good   High   Very high

6. *Multiple stores*
   Knowledge of the structure of multiple stores and of the advantages and disadvantages of using them as a channel of distribution.

   None   Some   Reasonable   Good   High   Very high

7. *Retail chains*
   Knowledge of the structure of retail chains and of the advantages and disadvantages of using them as a channel of distribution.

   None   Some   Reasonable   Good   High   Very high

8. *Department stores*
   Knowledge of the structure of department stores and of the advantages and disadvantages of using them as a channel of distribution.

   None   Some   Reasonable   Good   High   Very high

9. *Co-operative societies*
   Knowledge of the structure of co-operative societies and of the advantages and disadvantages of using them as a channel of distribution.

   None   Some   Reasonable   Good   High   Very high

10. *Supermarkets*
    Knowledge of the structure of supermarkets and of the advantages and disadvantages of using them as a channel of distribution.

    None   Some   Reasonable   Good   High   Very high

11. *Hypermarkets*
    Knowledge of the structure of hypermarkets and of the advantages and disadvantages of using them as a channel of distribution.

    None   Some   Reasonable   Good   High   Very high

12. *Cash and carry*
    Knowledge of the structure of cash and carry outlets and of the advantages and disadvantages of using them as a channel of distribution.

    None   Some   Reasonable   Good   High   Very high

13. *Discount stores*
    Knowledge of the structure of discount stores and of the advantages and disadvantages of using them as a channel of distribution.

    None   Some   Reasonable   Good   High   Very high

14. *Mobile retailers*
    Knowledge of the structure of mobile retailers and of the advantages and disadvantages of using them as a channel of distribution.

    None   Some   Reasonable   Good   High   Very high

15. *Van selling outlets*
    Knowledge of the structure of van selling outlets and of the advantages and disadvantages of using them as a channel of distribution.

    None   Some   Reasonable   Good   High   Very high

16. *Door-to-door selling*
    Knowledge of the structure of door-to-door selling and of the advantages and disadvantages of using it as a channel of distribution.

    None   Some   Reasonable   Good   High   Very high

17. *Garages*
    Knowledge of the structure of garages as retail outlets and of the advantages and disadvantages of using them as a channel of distribution.

    None   Some   Reasonable   Good   High   Very high

18. *Franchising*
    Knowledge of franchising and of the advantages and disadvantages of using it as a channel of distribution.

    None   Some   Reasonable   Good   High   Very high

19. *Party plan selling*
    Knowledge of party plan selling and of the advantages and disadvantages of using it as a channel of distribution.

    None   Some   Reasonable   Good   High   Very high

20. *Mail order*
    Knowledge of mail order and of the advantages and disadvantages of using it as a channel of distribution.

    None   Some   Reasonable   Good   High   Very high

21. *The commodity market*
    Knowledge of the commodity market and of the advantages and disadvantages of using it as a channel of distribution.

    None   Some   Reasonable   Good   High   Very high

22. *Agents, brokers and merchants*
    Knowledge of the use of agents, brokers and merchants and of the advantages and disadvantages of their use.

    None   Some   Reasonable   Good   High   Very high

23. *Exporting*
    Knowledge of the techniques and management of export distribution.

    None   Some   Reasonable   Good   High   Very high

24. *Industrial distribution*
    Knowledge of the techniques and management of industrial distribution.

    None   Some   Reasonable   Good   High   Very high

Warehouse Operation and Management

25. *Load unitisation*
    Understanding of the various methods of creating unit loads and of the principles of unit load design.

    None   Some   Reasonable   Good   High   Very high

26. *Utilisation of the warehouse cube*
    Understanding of the variables involved in obtaining the most economic utilisation of the warehouse cube, with the following elements:

    • *Pallet block storage*

    None   Some   Reasonable   Good   High   Very high

- *Palletised random access storage*

  None   Some   Reasonable   Good   High   Very high

- *High bay pallet silos*

  None   Some   Reasonable   Good   High   Very high

- *Minimisation of movement*

  None   Some   Reasonable   Good   High   Very high

27. *Paperwork efficiency*
    Knowledge of the principles and practice of obtaining optimum paperwork efficiency in warehousing.

    None   Some   Reasonable   Good   High   Very high

28. *Receiving and despatch*
    Knowledge of the principles and practice of the design and use of load/unload facilities.

    None   Some   Reasonable   Good   High   Very high

Managing Transport Services

29. *Vehicle plan*
    Understanding of the key aspects in developing a vehicle plan, in particular:

    - The need for vehicles at all.
    - Road, rail, air?
    - If road vehicles, own fleet or haulier?
    - If own fleet then lease, contract hire or purchase?
    - If company owned then how many, what type, where based, how financed?

    None   Some   Reasonable   Good   High   Very high

30. *Operator licensing*
    Knowledge of operator licensing and its conditions.

    None   Some   Reasonable   Good   High   Very high

31. *Vehicle management*
    Knowledge of the principles and practice of vehicle management with the following elements.

    - *Vehicle preparation*

    None   Some   Reasonable   Good   High   Very high

- *Vehicle loading and unloading*

  None   Some   Reasonable   Good   High   Very high

- *Vehicle running time management*

  None   Some   Reasonable   Good   High   Very high

- *Delivery management*

  None   Some   Reasonable   Good   High   Very high

32. *Drivers' hours and records*
    Knowledge of the statutory and managerial aspects of drivers' hours and records.

    None   Some   Reasonable   Good   High   Very high

33. *Vehicle selection and specification*
    Knowledge of the principles of vehicle selection and of the specification of purpose-built vehicles.

    None   Some   Reasonable   Good   High   Very high

34. *Vehicle acquisition*
    Knowledge of the alternative ways of acquiring a vehicle fleet and of the economics of choosing the appropriate way.

    None   Some   Reasonable   Good   High   Very high

35. *Vehicle maintenance*
    Knowledge of the principles and practice of developing a vehicle maintenance policy and managing it.

    None   Some   Reasonable   Good   High   Very high

36. *Financial control*
    Knowledge of the principles and practice of financial control of the transport function.

    None   Some   Reasonable   Good   High   Very high

37. *Costing*
    Knowledge of the principles and practice of costing transport operations.

    None   Some   Reasonable   Good   High   Very high

38. *Personnel transport*
    Knowledge of the issues involved in the transport of personnel.

    None   Some   Reasonable   Good   High   Very high

39. *Replacement policies*
    Knowledge of the issues involved in devising a cost-effective replacement policy for vehicles.

    None   Some   Reasonable   Good   High   Very high

40. *Company air services*
    Knowledge of the issues involved in planning the use of owned, leased, or bought-in company air services.

    None   Some   Reasonable   Good   High   Very high